THE REST
of
YOUR LIFE

Finding Repose in the Beloved

"If only I could give this book to everyone living in this modern age of go-go-go; John-Roger's wisdom in The Rest of Your Life taught me how to relax, let go and enjoy each moment. I was replenished and filled with a joy and fullness beyond words."

Jaime King
Actress

"The keys Drs. John-Roger and Paul Kaye bring to a more productive, balanced, and stress-free way of life are simple. We need only manage our attention and our energy – disentangling ourselves from what has them trapped and being more conscious about where and how they are directed. The authors walk their talk."

David Allen
Author, Getting Things Done: The Art of Stress-Free Productivity

"In our increasingly wired universe the hardest thing is finding ways to disentangle ourselves from the world and connect with our being. The Rest Of Your Lifeis an invaluable guide to the calm and clarity at the center of who we are."

Arianna Huffington
Editor and Chief, HuffingtonPost

About the Book

If you knew how to rest would you do it? Genuinely resting provides a variety of benefits, from improving health to enhancing your connection with who you truly are. Yet surprisingly few people know how to rest. John-Roger and Paul Kaye have made it easy to gain a greater understanding of what rest really is, how it works, and, most importantly, how to use it as a resource for accessing your inner essence, even in the midst of today's mad rush, multi-tasking environment.

As with all their books, The Rest of Your Life is eminently practical. It provides bite-sized and easy to absorb discussions that are brimming with usable wisdom, thoughts to reflect upon, and techniques to put into practice. However, don't get the idea that you will come away loaded down with new things you have to do. The experience of reading this book, whether going through it in sequence or just picking a page at random from time to time, is surprisingly... restful. This ease of use is also reflected in the companion CD, which is included with the book. It offers short meditations and reflections that can be enjoyed in just moments at a time.

Interspersed throughout the book are page-long sections titled "10 ways to restore Your Energy." With themes like The Breath, The Nap, Be Still, The Pause, and Resting in the Beloved, they put a new spin on some old, even ancient, ideas that will help you put your mind and body at ease.

With rest and relaxation having become increasingly scarce commodities, The Rest of Your Life is your lifeline to health, happiness and genuinely greater fulfillment.

Other Books by John-Roger, D.S.S.

Blessings of Light

The Consciousness of Soul

Divine Essence

Dream Voyages

Forgiveness - The Key to the Kingdom

Fulfilling Your Spiritual Promise

God Is Your Partner

Inner Worlds of Meditation

Journey of a Soul

Living Love from the Spiritual Heart

Loving Each Day

Loving Each Day for Moms and Dads

Loving Each Day for Peacemakers

Manual on Using The Light

Passage Into Spirit

The Path to Mastership

The Power Within You

Psychic Protection

Relationships: Love, Marriage and Spirit

Sex, Spirit and You

The Spiritual Family

Spiritual High (with Michael McBay)

The Spiritual Promise

Spiritual Warrior: The Art of Spiritual Living

Tao of Spirit

Timeless Wisdoms: Volume One

Walking With the Lord

The Way Out

Wealth and Higher Consciousness

When Are You Coming Home? (with Pauli Sanderson)

Other Books by John-Roger, D.S.S. and Paul Kaye, D.S.S.

Momentum: Letting Love Lead

What's It Like Being You?

www.mandevillepress.org

THE REST
of
YOUR LIFE

Finding Repose in the Beloved

JOHN-ROGER, D.S.S.

with PAUL KAYE, D.S.S.

Mandeville Press
Los Angeles, California

Mandeville Press
P.O. Box 513935
Los Angeles, CA 90051-1935
323-737-4055
jrbooks@mandevillepress.org
www.mandevillepress.org

Printed in the United States of America
ISBN# 978-1-893020-43-6

Photography by David Sand
Book design by Shelley Noble
Text set in Clearview font

Contents

The greatest secret is that the journey is already over before it has begun. You are already there. That one for whom you seek is already present.

Why is this a secret?

Because so few claim it.

Do you?

With your next breath?

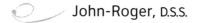 John-Roger, D.S.S.

There seems no plan because it's all plan.
There seems no center because it's all center.

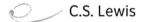 C.S. Lewis

A thousand years ago when they built the gardens
of Kyoto, the stones were set in the streams askew.
Whoever went quickly would fall in. When we slow,
the garden can choose what we notice. Can change
our heart.

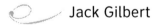 Jack Gilbert

Acknowledgments

Our thanks and appreciation go to the following whose time and loving energy brought this book about. Vincent Dupont who shepherded this book from its inception to its completion. Stephen Keel whose refined touches help to shape it. Nancy O'Leary, Carrie Hopkins, and Virginia Rose who generously volunteered their time to edit and proofread. As always, Laren Bright was on hand to cheerfully give his input and contribute to the copy. Special gratitude goes to Jsu Garcia who was first to read the initial draft and whose enthusiasm carried it through to completion, and to Angel Gibson and Betsy Alexander for their constant support.

Foreword

The keys to a more productive, balanced, and stress-free way of life are simple. We need only manage our attention and our energy—disentangling ourselves from what has them trapped and being more conscious about where and how they are directed.

For many years a consultant and educator in the arena of personal productivity, I have worked closely with some of the brightest, busiest, and most successful people in the world. Without exception, their opportunities for improvement have been the ones we all have—reducing distractions and applying appropriate focus.

To manage ourselves, we need control and perspective. The more we feel out of control, driven by our circumstances, the more we experience the angst of the victim, with its resulting over-reactivity or numbness. And the more we lose sight of what's real and what matters, the more we suffer the unease of only partial engagement with ourselves and our world.

Though control and focus are keys, they are also the villains. It is our attempts to control our world and our inability to let go of our focus that create unnecessary stress and limit our abilities to perform at our highest rate. So in a strange way, what seems like the thing to do is the very thing that trips us up. When we feel like the world gets bigger than we are we try to get a tighter hold on it. And the harder we try to "control" things in that way, the more out of control we become. And when the cup of personal fulfillment feels less than full, we feel compelled to look harder and more frenetically "out there," and satisfaction eludes us.

These errors in approach are ultimately self-correcting. Trying to control what can't be controlled and trying to satisfy ourselves with what inherently does not satisfy leads in time to unwanted negative experiences that will teach us, in spite of ourselves. Pain can be a great educator. But inspiration can be, too. If you're like me, and prefer the latter course, you'll appreciate this remarkable little book.

What follows is a wealth of golden nuggets that can be catalysts to remembering the really good stuff you probably already know. There are also plenty of practical tips for making that knowledge useful, right away. The message is not to disengage from an active life, but to align it and implement effective strategies. Having known and worked with both John-Roger and Paul Kaye in various capacities for more than three decades, I can attest that the authors walk this talk. They marry intelligence, integrity, and deep experience with a tireless dedication to assisting people achieve the freedm that these keys bring. Don't be surprised if you find, as I have, a special energy that comes through their writing, beyond the words.

Completion and cooperation provide the control I'm after —not working harder. And when I stop, look, and listen—putting my attention into the places that are the real source of my creativity—I achieve the focus that fulfills. I'm grateful that *The Rest of Your Life* is now here as a tool to keep close at hand, when I need those reminders.

David Allen
Ojai, California
August 2007
Author, *Getting Things Done: the Art of Stress-Free Productivity*

Just
sit there right now.
Don't do a thing. Just rest.

For your
separation from God
is the hardest work in this world.

 Hafiz

Introduction

Come to me, all you who are weary and
burdened, and I will give you rest.

Matthew 11:28 NIV

You may be the type of person who tells yourself that you need to get away in order to rest or that you will rest when you have time. Perhaps you say that when the job or project is done, then you'll rest. Maybe you are even waiting for "the kids to be grown up" before you'll rest. This way of living life, where we are consistently putting off what is essential for us, makes no rational sense at all. Rest is already in our presence and the purpose of this book is to assist you in making the crucial, subtle shift that enables you to fully experience rest in at least one of its many facets.

There are many ways of looking at what rest actually is. It can be the refreshing and centered feeling after a good night's rest, a moment of ease after something is completed, or the feeling of relief from what troubles or disturbs us.

Rest is also a period of inactivity, often tranquil, that can be taken in solitude. Rest can be a wave of quiet spiritual calm when our mind ceases its activity for an instant. Rest is the absence of motion and also the interval of silence between notes in music. We rest when we take a short pause from our activity or journey. Not only do we rest when we are relaxed, still, and when we give up our burdens. Also, the defense rests its case and our eyes rest on someone we love.

It is not only a multifaceted word but also, in life, a richly nuanced expression—an attitude that we can bring into our daily lives, no matter what we are doing. Life is made up of individual moments. There is no need to wait to rest when we can rest right now in the moment or between moments. In this book, we are attempting to show you that it isn't necessary to strain in order to live life. As counterintuitive as it may seem in today's culture, for the most part life can be lived in a relaxed, restful way. Since life is primarily breathing in and breathing out, perhaps we can even learn to rest in between breaths.

In the sport of pistol shooting, an Olympic event, the competitor needs to hit a very small target with an outstretched arm. It is necessary that the arm be very still, as even a heartbeat is enough to move the pistol off its intended target. Any excitement in the competitor must be reduced to a minimum as the effect of adrenaline can cause a subtle shaking of the hand. All that matters is stillness and focus. Shooters, while removing themselves from any emotion, must still be completely present with hitting the target, combining a clear intention with inner rest and stillness. Thus the pistol is shot between heartbeats.

The practitioner of Tai Chi Chuan (a Chinese martial art), when "pushing hands," (a cooperative form of sparring) must be completely relaxed to send his opponent off balance. The tense person is easily pushed away. The most successful person at pushing hands is the most relaxed. Not surprisingly, Tai Chi Chuan has proven itself to be excellent for health.

As far back as 300 B.C., the philosopher Chuang Tzu observed that when an archer was practicing, he shot with relaxation and skill. When a moderate financial award was placed in front of the archer, he got a little tense, his aim faltered, and he often missed the target. When a large award was offered for his accuracy, he became nervous and worried, with obvious results. This led Chuang Tzu to wryly observe that, "He who looks too hard on the outside gets clumsy on the inside."

In modern times people who play golf find their swing is near perfect when there is no ball to hit. But once a ball is placed on the tee and someone is keeping score, the inexperienced golfer's swing inevitably fails and the ball goes off its intended path. When a golfer has a "drink," he often becomes more relaxed and his game improves. So even though a specific feat can be improved by artificial means, it is at the expense of our being fully present and reduces our ability to respond to other circumstances. Imagine how our performance in everyday life would improve if we could learn to find rest and relaxation from within ourselves.

The question is, "How could we relax in the process of living?" or, "How can we have rest in our daily lives? How do we live for the rest of our lives?" This book is a series of reflections on the theme of finding rest and relaxation, peace and tranquility, within ourselves and within the great Self that embraces and holds us all.

Incorporating rest and relaxation as a response to daily life is a learned habit. It's an awake and aware state that is able to respond appropriately when the moment of action arrives. There is no need to respond needlessly before that moment. A common example of a needless response is worry, which is a waste of our precious life energy.

Rest is also the ability to turn off and renew ourselves. One of the reasons stress continues to cause wear and tear and sickness is because, increasingly, we don't know when to turn off. Even when people leave their jobs at the end of the day, many continue to "work" just below their conscious awareness. That "work" is usually the worry or preoccupation with what needs to be done or completed in their lives. Adding to that are the concerns for loved ones and the pressure to simply keep up with appearances—maintaining a youthful face and body, or just trying to keep pace with the neighbor's materiality. It is a slow, inexorable path towards physical, mental, and emotional exhaustion.

Yet, thank goodness, there is an antidote—an alternative way to live for the rest of our lives. It's free, already present within us, and immediately available. As you read through these pages, allow yourself to find repose in the Beloved—for the rest of your life.

This book is designed to be read in any way your heart desires—from beginning to end or starting at the middle. You can open the book at a random page and gain inspiration for the day or for a problem that you are working through.

This being human is a guest house.
Every morning a new arrival.

A joy, a depression, a meanness,
some momentary awareness comes
as an unexpected visitor.

Welcome and entertain them all!
Even if they're a crowd of sorrows,
who violently sweep your house
empty of its furniture,
still, treat each guest honorably.
He may be clearing you out
for some new delight.

Rumi, "The Guest House"

So Simple, So Ordinary

A big part of my work with people has been to demonstrate to them that they are divine through stories, metaphors, the updating of the esoteric teachings of old, and above all personal experience. To show them that no matter what they do, the spark of divinity lies within them waiting to be awakened through their loving attention.

Many people "get it" and then they fall out of it again. Most people don't get it at all because they use their bodies, mind, and emotions as a reference point and compare themselves to others. By judging themselves and others, they miss the whole point.

I have often wondered how they can miss what is immediately present within them, closer to them than their next breath. It may be because they feel that their divinity has to manifest as some radiant light, that they need to be able to heal people with a look, or somehow levitate. While it is true that spiritually we do radiate and are known through our level of Light, in this physical day-to-day world, our divinity mostly expresses through our ordinariness.

When we are knocked down by life's storms and we get back up again, we are exercising our divinity. When we choose to love rather than judge, we are exercising our divinity. When we withhold the blow rather than needlessly strike out, we are exercising our divinity. Our divinity therefore is demonstrated in our ordinary moment-to-moment choices

The dark thought, the shame, the malice,
meet them at the door laughing,
and invite them in.

Be grateful for whoever comes,
because each has been sent
as a guide from beyond.

Rumi, "The Guest House"

It's All a Blessing

I have a friend who fell and broke his femur (thigh bone). It was very debilitating for him and, needing to spend months in a wheelchair, he got quite depressed. A good friend of his who was visiting him in the hospital told him, "Now is the time to use everything you know." He used the year in recovery to make new discoveries, re-examine his life, and develop a new and more interesting vocation. When he told me this story, I said that his accident turned out to be a wonderful blessing. He looked at me intensely and said, "No! I made it a blessing."

I realized that he was showing me a great truth. He was exercising his divinity to make a positive choice and change the pathway of his life. He used what happened to him for his upliftment, learning, and growth. He used the experience as a stepping stone instead of a stumbling block. When we do this, we manifest the divine. To stay a victim, to judge ourselves, or others, or the state of the world, exercises our ego and personality; it does not exercise our divinity.

So, lighten up. Get a sense of humor about life. Your destiny isn't some vague, romantic future; it is what is right in front of you right now. Use what you've got and what you know. You are divine. Learn to manifest joy under any conditions. There is much to celebrate.

I believe Icarus was not failing as he fell,
but just coming to the end of his triumph.

Jack Gilbert

Why Not Tell Ourselves the Good Stuff

We are in "that which is" all the time. It's reality. When we declare "that which is" to be something else, the result is a feeling of separation and loneliness. Yet we are the ones who create that feeling. Instead of accepting and cooperating and facing what is, we turn away and blame someone or something because we are not getting what we want.

We are the ones in charge and responsible for our lives. The Beloved is always present waiting for us to return to it through our attention and awareness. We can dissolve the separation instantly if we can just stop empowering our thoughts of separation and our feelings of inadequacy through playing the victim.

Our bodies build their form around the energy we place out. If we misuse our energy by putting our attention in the wrong place, the body will build its form around it. For example, if you worry a lot, it will be reflected in your tense shoulders and your tight stomach. When we start to use our energy correctly, our shoulders loosen, the stomach relaxes, the energy starts moving into the areas that have been blocked or closed off, and the body starts aligning itself spontaneously. Correct use of energy makes everything liquid, relaxed, and smooth. The body will line itself up and re-form itself according to your conscious thought and pattern of behavior.

The lesson is that if we don't change our behavior, the body will go back to its previous condition. If we are willing to listen and watch, we'll find that the body is not only educating us in how to get well but also showing us how to change the condition that produced the sense of imbalance or illness.

We condition ourselves by what we tell ourselves. We actually tell ourselves what we don't really want or need to hear—how we are a failure, we don't feel good or look good, nothing is working, and that our life is going to hell. It's so funny because if we can tell ourselves the bad stuff, surely we can tell ourselves the good stuff. After all, we are the ones making up the stories, so why not tell ourselves stories that will lift us and move us into greater loving? We are in charge of what we say to ourselves. We can say that our lives are full of health, wealth, and happiness; abundance, prosperity, and riches; loving, caring, and sharing; and the joy of touching to others with that fullness. That story is closer to the truth of who you are and will manifest for you because, as you think in your heart, you will become.

We have what we seek.
It is there all the time,
and if we slow down and be still,
it will make itself known to us.

Thomas Merton

Just Now. Only Now.

A great deal of the stress that people suffer is a result of not living right now—of being occupied with the past or the future. This is the cause of so many troubles. When you cut out your concern for the future and your remembrance of the past, you are right here, now.

Many people try to remember to be here now. However, when they try to remember, the very act of remembering throws them out of the present moment. If you stop remembering, or you forget to remember, and you are just here now, you are in good territory.

Do your best to maintain your attention in the now. There is nothing else in existence other than right now. As you handle life as it appears moment-by-moment, you find out that everything is fine, smooth, and right where it should be.

In fact, you don't want to jump off into the future because right now is really quite nice. There is no past or future. Being present connects you with the eternal now and there is only one way to go—up in consciousness.

The solution to life's challenges is really quite simple. To get yourself back into the presence of the Beloved, move into the present moment, and love whatever is happening in and around you.

Resting Point: Ways to Restore Your Energy

*I love being alive. I really do.
And I think the way the world is going to
transform is by us getting back in touch with
the joy of being alive for its own sake.*

Matt Sanford

The Breath. Your breath is one of your greatest allies. It is the key to restoring your energy. It is mentioned a lot in this book, but here are some keys and reminders:

Just the simple act of following the rising and falling of your breath can bring you to a peaceful and calm place and restore your energy. It also brings you into the ever-present, but often elusive, now.

Allowing the breath into the belly is one of the best things you can do to reduce stress.

The key to natural and full breathing is in the exhalation—the letting go. However, don't force anything. As you observe the exhale, you may be aware of a slight pause. This is natural, just observe. Then, without forcing anything, open to receive the next breath into you.

Place the breath anywhere in your body where you have tension, anywhere it feels lifeless or numb. You may find that as you bring the breath into that part of your body,what felt "dead" starts to come "alive."

Sometimes I lie awake at night and ask,

"Where have I gone wrong?"

Then a voice says to me,

"This is going to take more than one night."

Charles M. Schulz

One of the Best Pieces of Advice I Can Give You

We're here with each other on this planet to love, to care, and to share. When you hear someone close to you being negative with themselves, you can tell them that they don't have to pick on themselves like that. They can move forward and start living their life from where they are. We are all doing that, anyway.

Jesus was born in a manger to show us that we start from where we are. You don't have to wait till you get to the king or queen's throne before you take off for your destiny.

One of the best pieces of advice that I can give you is to start from where you are, right now. Don't try to repair anything, don't try to fix anything, don't try to change anything. Let this moment be the starting point, right here, right now, and just go up from this point.

In your own bosom you have your heaven and earth,
all you behold though it appears without, it is within.

William Blake

Why Don't I Know It?

The body ages, the emotions go up and down, and the mind keeps playing games. So we know from direct experience that these levels are transitory. Their value is moving through them and holding your spiritual inner awareness as the constant in your life in the eternity of each moment. Eternity is *now* for all time. It was *now* when this book was written, and it is *now* when you are reading it.

Now is eternity, and that is the place to keep bringing your awareness. You do this by releasing the conditioned energy that you have placed around you through the roles you play. To function in this world, we all play roles: one moment we are the shopper, then the lover, then the teacher, the wife driving the car, or the husband taking out the garbage. All is well until we forget that it is a role and we get caught up when we identify with it and think we are the role we play. Then, strangely, we defend it and fight for it. At best your role is an extension of you, but to identify yourself fully as the role is to condition yourself into separation.

Separation has been built into the conditioning of mankind. It is known esoterically as the "fall" of consciousness. But in the higher awareness, it is an illusion. For we of the Spirit know that we can get up one more time than we fall. As we do that the conditioning is broken and we can choose, once again, to turn our attention to the Beloved and know we are home. We extend ourselves into the Beloved and replace our conditioning with our knowing. That is the true power within each of us.

Knowing we are the Beloved gives us a new reference point through which we can then know the transcendental nature of Spirit and reach within to the Soul, the God force.

Ancient lovers believed a kiss would
literally unite their souls, because the
spirit was said to be carried in one's breath.

Eve Glicksman

The Natural Process of Life

Life is divine communion. It's an eternal process that breathes in and breathes out. This process of life is present, now. What makes it all so very nice is that there is only God, and God is present in your consciousness, directly. Knowing that then, you can participate in the divine communion of life by physically experiencing the fullness and "realities" of the world without identifying with them. As you move through the world you use your emotions to enhance your experience and your mind to select and direct you in your activities. These are tools to place those things that come to you in the right perspective so that you can recognize the divine essence that is the Soul in all things.

Divine communion is being loving. It's that quality by which you experience yourself dancing in your own heart. It's where the sacred sounds sing in your heart. Not saying the sacred tones in your mind, but hearing them resounding in your heart and through every part of your being as you ride on the bliss of your own true nature; that is participating in your own divine communion.

At the moment of communion with your own being, your consciousness automatically expands. An analogy is that when you breathe out, breathing in is automatic. That's the process of life. So you don't try to expand your consciousness. You can't do it by trying. You expand your consciousness by making yourself available to Spirit, to the Beloved, by your willingness to be open and present within that total loving presence of God.

When you are in divine communion, you may find yourself moving very naturally into the stream of Light we call the Sound Current of God.

Resting Point: Ways to Restore Your Energy

There is more refreshment and stimulation
in a nap, even of the briefest,
than in all the alcohol ever distilled.

Ovid

The Nap. Napping is one of nature's great gifts to us. It is very underutilized in our culture. Twenty minutes is ideal but even a five-minute nap can be very restorative. But don't go longer than twenty minutes as it is likely you will move into a deeper stage of sleep and instead of feeling refreshed upon awakening, you may feel groggy.

There is no doubt that our culture is sleep-deprived. Don't be a victim to all the demands of life. You have a marvelous tool at your disposal for restoring your energy—napping.

If you only have a minute, try this. Hold some keys in your hands and bend forward in your chair with your lower arms resting on your thighs. As you nod off, the keys will drop and wake you up. Even in that minute, you will feel a little more refreshed.

The point here is that taking a little time for yourself for rest, prayer, meditation, or spiritual exercises, can profoundly affect the quality of your day.

When we make music, we don't do it
in order to reach a certain point,
such as the end of the composition.
If that were the purpose of music,
then obviously the fastest players
would be the best. Also, when we are
dancing, we are not aiming to arrive at a
particular place on the floor as in a journey.
When we dance, the journey itself is the
point, as when we play music, the playing
itself is the point. And exactly the same
thing is true in meditation. Meditation is
the discovery that the point of life is always
arrived at in the immediate moment.

Alan Watts

Patience

You can perceive your very breathing process as a form of patience. What would happen if you tried to take all the rest of your breaths right now? You'd probably explode. It would be too much to handle. So you take them one after another, in their proper timing. You let your breathing take care of itself, knowing that it is set up to do just that. And, without any effort, you're pretty patient toward that process. For the most part, the breaths are taken gradually. You can speed them up, but then you get the results of that, too, which might be too much energy and a little hyperventilation. So you then slow the breathing down to bring it into a balance.

In every season there is a rhythm, and in every person there is a rhythm. This rhythm has an innate intelligence that naturally moves and flows with what is going on. When you can tune into your inner rhythm (maybe for you it's a concerto, a waltz, or a march), you can sense its flow and relax into it. You then live a divine melody.

As you sit and listen to your rhythm within, you can amplify it, and build on it to create the beautiful symphony that truly represents the divine spark of God within you. But it needs to be done gradually within the rhythm that is very particularly yours.

The sound inside of you is the Sound of God. But sometimes, when you are distracted by the difficulties in your world, you won't pause long enough to listen to the sound and the assistance coming from within you. When you have a difficulty or feel stuck, you can start the attunement to Spirit by chanting "Hu" (pronounced like hue) or "Ani-Hu" (pronounced ahn-eye hue).

Best of all is to preserve everything
in a pure, still heart, and let there be
for every pulse a thanksgiving,
and for every breath a song.

Konrad von Gesner

Beyond the Fields of Illusion

Your heart doesn't stop beating when you aren't aware of it. And if you focus your awareness on your breath, you may take in more air, expand the chest, and wake up a little, but that doesn't mean that you would stop breathing if you weren't paying attention to the process. Your mind is not in charge of the process.

Neither does the mind help you in opening to the Beloved, for spiritual awakening bypasses the mind. If you tend to be mental in your approach, you might be able to get intellectual pleasure in comprehending the process, but don't confuse that with spiritual understanding. You may tend to substitute a pleasurable past experience or focus on the future, especially if you are going through difficulties now. Although it might feel good, you are not living right here and now.

You can't get to tomorrow without going through today. It is possible to experience joy and humor even during difficult times. It depends upon your attitude and altitude today. The joy of Spirit is present in all times, difficult or easy. It's not necessary to hold on to what happened yesterday or put energy into concern about tomorrow. Be all of you, in all of today. Let the past be what it is—over and done with. Let tomorrow take care of itself by completing what is in front of today.

As you walk the path of the Beloved, you will come across the illusionary fields from time to time. They are nothing to be overly concerned about. Just move across them and back into the realities of the Spirit. You can transform the energy forms of the world by breathing the divine energy in and out. Your breath will move you through the fields of illusions and lift you higher.

Zov, a peasant, tells his wife,
"If I were the Czar, I would be richer
than the Czar!"

"How," she asks.

"I would take in a little
sewing on the side."

Old Jewish joke

Relax. Be Light-Hearted

When we are tense, we hold on to what isn't there. We tend to fight and resist as a way of showing strength. Living this way is more a sign of weakness. Relaxing and letting go demonstrate true strength.

When you are relaxed, you are more sensitive and aware. You know not to react when someone says something potentially upsetting or negative. You have the presence to say inside of you one very effective word, "deflect." This single word can work wonders against a verbal or psychic attack.

There is no need to give up your center for someone else's upset or let negativity build in or around you. It can be handled in a relaxed way.

If someone pushes against you physically, emotionally, or mentally, yield and let go. Don't be there. Be on the other side of them. Be like a revolving door, one door gives as you push, the other follows behind.

In this way, you preserve the quality of relaxation. If you find yourself starting to be stubborn or resistant, better to give up your position than lose the quality of relaxation and centeredness in order to preserve that position.

The basic principle of letting go, of relaxation, will produce a softness and kindness in your demeanor. Others will often mistake that kindness for weakness. So be light-hearted, good humored, and let there be vitality in your relaxation. Resistance, like tension, is just opposing something that is, in reality, not there. You may feel justified in your opposition but it is really a strike against yourself. When you get right down to the core of it, we are only upset with ourselves.

Silence is not just not talking.

It's a place where all things come from. All voices, all creation comes out of this silence. So when you're standing on the edge of silence, you hear things you've never heard before, and you hear things in ways you've never heard them before.

John Francis

The Best Course

The best course is to stay in your loving. There is absolutely no need to play the game that you are no good, or that you are not worthy. It's a fool's game. Claim that you are divine and allow yourself to soar in that awareness. Do not fear who you are. Relax into your very cells and know you have everything you need in this moment.

When you feel tension, let go of your resistance. When you feel life is too hard, stop pushing. When you stop the push, you may feel less tired. Are you pushing to get hold of something that is not yours and never will be?

If you can stop for a moment in your thinking and your questing and listen to the silence, you may start becoming aware of many levels of consciousness and that you are a multi-dimensional being existing on all levels simultaneously. The trick is to learn to shift your awareness to where you wish to be.

Those who sit very quietly in the silence that roars the name of the Lord, and do the most mundane jobs in love and devotion, are performing a beautiful service that God sees as very great indeed.

Start living now.

Stop saving the good china for
that special occasion. Stop withholding
your love until that special person
materializes. Every day you are alive
is a special occasion. Every minute,
every breath, is a gift from God.

Mary Manin Morrissey

In the Quiet

Take time to just be quiet. To sit and allow the body to become still, the emotions to let go, and the mind to relax—to just be. Nothing has to be present and obvious to you through the perceptions of your mind, emotions, and body. Let yourself move from the sensual awareness of the outer world to the being awareness of where your breath is coming from—where your existence originates. As you relax into that prior condition, you are in a state of truth.

As we become close to others, they may wrap their expectations around us. The striving to fulfill them can cause us to empty from our being and move into theirs, and we lose our freedom. We separate our consciousness from the love, and the result is pain. This prevents us from knowing the transcendental nature of now.

There are false states along the path towards truth. The false states are the ego states, the illusions, and the romance of "I love God, God loves me. God will take care of me." Then something untoward happens, and you say, "What happened to God? He didn't take care of me!" He is taking care of you; you are still breathing. Maybe you had something else in mind, like roses or dollar bills, but breathing is all that is really going on. As soon as you can move to that which is going on and forget the wishful thinking or the hopeful plans of what you want to take place, the further along you will be on the path of reality.

The Spirit within you is the same Spirit within everything. There truly is no separation. You have the freedom to live your life the way you see as right and proper, and you stay free by allowing and extending that freedom to everyone.

*You have not to do anything in
the positive sense of the word,
in order to realize God. Simply
undo what you have done in the
way of making your prison house,
and there you are, God already,
Truth personified already.*

Sawan Singh

God Is Here, Now.

In order to see the face of God, take a moment to let go and, for a moment, permit yourself to perceive past the illusions and conditioning of this world and this society. Even see past the illusion of your own senses and past your own dilemmas and the problems you create. Move inwardly into a neutral place where there is no attachment to results or to the process of getting someplace. It's enough that you're present, enjoying things around you as they are. No matter what anyone else does, continue to express from your loving heart.

Realize that God is present in everything. God is entirely present, all the time. Perhaps your predicament in life is simply your misunderstanding of the absolute "hereness" and "nowness" of God's presence.

Take a moment to find the harmony within you. Rest there even if it is only for a split second. Life is as simple as breathing in and breathing out, and once you find the rhythm of that, you can follow it through. If you could practice just that simple discipline and maintain it, you would start overcoming all of this physical world.

To find harmony you can always begin by getting out of the past. There is absolutely no need to think about yesterday or last week. Just tell yourself to stop doing that. Don't waste time thinking about tomorrow; forget it. Do nothing except—right now—feel where your body is, feel your feet on the ground. Take in a deep breath. Enjoy that breath and as you let it out, release the strain from yourself. Receive of the next breath and let it go. All that is necessary right now is to follow your breathing. You are present with yourself in the most simple, unadorned, and complete way.

Resting Point: Ways to Restore Your Energy

Learning how to be still, to really be still and let life happen—that stillness becomes a radiance.

Morgan Freeman

Slow Down. Experiment with moving more slowly and more consciously. Stay purposeful but take your time. For many people, time is a scarcer commodity these days so there is a tendency to rush to fit everything in. Slowing down may be counterintuitive when it appears that so much needs to be done, but actually you'll be surprised as to how much more can be accomplished.

Look at it this way—2,600 years ago, Aesop wrote a fable about a race between the tortoise and the hare. If you have forgotten who won, here is a clue—it wasn't the hare.

There is no reality except the one contained within us. That is why so many people live such an unreal life. They take the images outside them for reality and never allow the inner world to assert itself.

Hermann Hesse

Seeing Perfectly by Seeing Directly

As you come into more continual communion with the Beloved, you may give the appearance of being in bliss. Your emotions are calm and your mind is content. You realize that you have everything you have wished for, inwardly. You are in a very balanced state of being.

As you touch into the Beloved more and more, you share this state of being with others, not by talking about it, but by example. As they see your light, they will start moving in the direction of their own light. The light in you will awaken the light in them. You don't have to do anything special to serve in this way, yet you are being of tremendous service when you are present in this dynamic, yet peaceful, state of being.

Yet you must be watchful for whenever you put other people down, you separate from the Beloved, and you will feel it. It's not others that you hurt with your words—your words really hurt you. They pull you into separation so no one can reach you. The situation is artificial because you are not really separate, but you have separated yourself through illusion and through your attitude.

Fortunately, it is so easy to get back into the oneness. Keep breathing naturally and, in the breathing in of the life force, you will start uniting within yourself again. As often as you find mistakes and fallacies in another personality, as many times as you fight and separate, is how often you can unite once again spiritually with the one from whom you separated.

In this way you can know your true being, which is not separated from you and never has been. You may have been conditioned to believing that man fell and was separated from God and that, in the separation, sin came into the world. But that too is artificial. It never really took place. The people who

believe that it took place don't have a big enough God and have separated themselves from the true God.

Maybe they have a God with a beard or they imagine God as an old man. However, the One that is eternal, the Beloved, is present in all things continuously.

*The transition from tenseness,
self-responsibility, and worry, to
equanimity, receptivity, and peace,
is the most wonderful of all those
shiftings of inner equilibrium, those
changes of the personal center of
energy;... and the chief wonder of it is
that it so often comes about, not by
doing, but by simply relaxing and
throwing the burden down.*

William James

Be on Your Own Side

It isn't life's events that cause stress, but it is our reaction to those events that activates the symptoms of stress. For the most part, stress is internally generated by our negative attitude towards ourselves and what is going on in life. The choice of our attitude, choosing between being tense or relaxed in a situation, can be made at any moment. You may thrive on the thrill of stress, but it is likely that there is an addiction to the surge of adrenaline. With practice you'll find that being completely present with whatever is going on is far more thrilling.

We lose nothing by slowing down. We find that by gaining our center and resting there, we can connect with the Beloved. When we get upset and annoyed, our attention shifts, and we let go of that precious connection. Why miss another moment to be with the Beloved, the truth of the heart? The moment we realize that the Beloved is entirely present, here and now will dissipate any upset and our energy will change to joy.

When we find that sacred center of our being, the spiritual energy starts radiating out of us and everything takes on an equal quality of humor in this divine comedy that we are all involved with. If we spill a bag of precious jewels, we pick them up and put them back. If we spill a load of fresh manure, we shovel it. From that sacred center they're both the same— they're both nothing. So you don't have to enter into the confusion of life at all. You can just sit and do absolutely nothing.

That moment of quiet—or nothingness—of silence, is when we find out that, inwardly, we are wealthy beyond measure. We're no longer hung up, but we're free and flowing and we joyously realize that, despite momentary appearances to the contrary, things have been moving our way all along.

The Spirit of God hath made me,
and the breath of the Almighty
hath given me life.

Job 33:4

Watching the Breath

"If my mind would just leave me alone..."

How can it leave you alone when you're tracking back over the wastelands of the past all the time? The mind is to be used today. It's an instrument of perception. The emotions are to be released from yesterday and used today. They're instruments of feeling. The mind and emotions are tools for perception, feeling, and action; these bring completion on this level. You truly accomplish something when you use these tools to complete this day. Jesus said, "Let the dead bury the dead." He was saying that the past is past; let it go. Live today. This moment is life.

The moments to come are just a "prospect" of life, and the moments past are memories. Leave the memories to others and come present in the reality of this breath. Many teachers say that a good technique for overcoming difficulties is to concentrate on your breathing and watch yourself breathe. That can be difficult to do, because breathing is such a habitual response that you forget to focus on it consciously. While you're watching your breathing, you start thinking, "I wonder if anybody else is watching their breathing? They're probably out playing golf." And instantly you're with them playing golf in your mind and forget that you're supposed to be watching your breathing.

It is important to hold your consciousness in the now, in the reality of each moment as it comes forward in space and time. In that precious present you can be honest, direct, and straightforward with the people you're with and allow the love and light of your consciousness to shine through.

If I were called upon to state in a few words the essence of everything I was trying to say both as a novelist and as a preacher, it would be something like this: Listen to your life. See it for the fathomless mystery that it is. In the boredom and pain of it, no less than in the excitement and gladness: touch, taste, smell your way to the holy and hidden heart of it, because in the last analysis, all moments are key moments, and life itself is grace.

Frederick Buechner

There Is Nothing to Fix

I am amazed at the capacity of us human beings, with our inherent divinity and endowed with intelligence and enormous abilities, to create our own problems. And one of the biggest problems we create is trying to fix ourselves. Yet there is nothing to be fixed.

Life is a learning process, each experience being a stepping stone to the next. And if we keep moving and letting go along the way, it leads us to expanded consciousness and awareness. But so often we don't let go. We stop moving so we can identify something as wrong and then we try to fix it. And it can't be fixed in our mind or with our emotions, and so we become confused. We turn to worry as a solution, when worry does nothing except make us sick. We judge ourselves, thinking that is a solution, when judging builds negative consequences for ourselves.

Let's not make trouble for ourselves. Why condemn or judge when we can live each day and see what is revealed to us? God is constantly supplying, and for us to be constantly receiving, we also have to be continually letting go. We have to let go of this breath to receive the next one.

It makes so much sense to let go, spiritually and healthwise, yet the human condition seems to urge us to hold on. We hold on to our positions, our need to be right, and our desire for respect or recognition. And we label our condition and then try to fix it. There is nothing to fix because it will clear itself, if we are willing to move on in our existence. Moving on can be as simple as a smile. Yes, that simple.

Resting Point: Ways to Restore Your Energy

Within you there is a stillness and a sanctuary to
which you can retreat at any time and be yourself.

Hermann Hesse

Be Still. Stillness is a much ignored and neglected gift that we have stowed away. Now is the time to bring it down from the loft and open this gift, so that we can now allow ourselves to receive its bounty.

Take a moment, right now, to just be still. It is useful to say to yourself, in a deep way, "Peace, be still." It's amazing how it can bring a wave of calm over us, and restore us.

The quote from Psalm 46:10, "Be still, and know that I am God," informs us that we can attune to God by the simple act of being still. If you are calling on God, I strongly suggest that you be still and listen. If you hear nothing and it's just still, realize that underneath the stillness is the Beloved, who is holding the stillness. In everything you do, whether it's a failure or a success, the Beloved contains and holds all of that.

So be still for even a minute. Say, "Peace, be still," and rest in the stillness.

It costs so much to be a full human
being that there are very few who have
the enlightenment or the courage to pay
the price.

One has to abandon altogether the
search for security and reach out to
the risk of living with both arms open.
One has to embrace the world like a lover.

Morris West

Letting Go of Insecurity

It is common for people to resist or be uncomfortable with change. It is human nature to look for security. Yet the only permanent thing on this planet is change. So much is changing so rapidly that we can no longer turn to what we used to rely upon to provide security. This places us in the only thing that is secure and that does not disappear—that which exists, that which is, that which is never born and never dies—who you truly are.

Who you truly are loves unconditionally. When your relationships are characterized by unconditional loving and acceptance, you'll find that your defenses are replaced by an openness that encourages sharing and release. You create a mutual, loving environment, without judgment, which is a powerful, spiritual place to be in.

In unconditional loving, strength and a sense of freedom beyond your wildest dreams is the natural outcome, and risk is no longer frightening. Transcendence of fear, pain, and guilt is possible. Discovering your inner peace is the surest, straightest path to finding that sense of security.

Freedom from stress, insecurity, and anxiety lies in loving yourself and accepting yourself unconditionally. From the dwelling of worth and peace within you, from that self-loving place, you will receive more loving and acceptance from those around you. When a person (whether it is a spouse, relative, friend, or business associate) is ready to accept you as unconditionally as you have accepted yourself, then you have a true relationship to invest in, a relationship with unlimited rewards.

Spiritual love, unconditional love says, "I love you, no matter what." This kind of love creates a harmonious balance

that encompasses the mental, emotional, and physical expressions of love. Where spiritual love is present, there is tremendous security. Neither person walks in fear of disappointing the other or being judged or criticized. There is loving acceptance of each other's strengths and frailties. When you achieve spiritual love with another, you will feel more alive than you ever have, and at the same time, more relaxed and joyous. There is not enough money or goods on the planet to buy the love I am talking about. Unconditional love is truly free.

*Give up to grace. The ocean takes care
of each wave till it gets to shore.*

Rumi

Living in Grace

Under the law of this world we must strive, but under Grace it is given unto us. When we are under Grace, all we need say is, "Lord, I receive," and what we need is given to us.

When we enter into negative patterns, we enter into the law of this world and must function under it. Yet as soon as we enter into unconditional loving, that loving is manifested and there is nothing we can do wrong in that purity—it is all right. For when Grace is extended to us, those things that have been out of balance in our lives can be balanced instantly.

Getting into the consciousness of Grace is very easy. It's so simple that people miss it because they think it should be harder. It's simply letting go and letting God. When you do let go and let God, it's done. But you do have to have the faith for a few seconds to truly let go.

To let go is to relax. And to let God is to be patient. So just relax and be patient. Let your love be your guiding star. Let it be in your breath. Then you live in the heart of God, all things are made new and the Beloved is personally present with you, all the time.

*Enlightenment is not imagining
figures of light but making the
darkness conscious.*

Carl Gustav Jung

The Enlightened Life

We are all working towards enlightenment. Perhaps you think enlightenment means that you know everything there is to know about anything there is to know. That may be a form of genius, but it is not enlightenment.

Enlightenment isn't somewhere in the future, "One day when I'm enlightened... Neither is enlightenment an end result; it is a process of forgiving everyone in your life as you move through it. Enlightenment is not a destination, it's a process—a way of behaving, of perceiving, of doing, of giving, of caring, where there is no blame and no punishment.

Having a receptive mind is part of enlightenment and giving is the key to enlightenment. Do you give or do you take? Enlightenment is not a bright light that shines and blinds everybody. Enlightenment is the process by which you relate to people in your conversation, in your daily occupation. One of the foremost things to look for in enlightenment is forgiveness.

That moment inside of you where you forgive what's happened is the moment when you are enlightening yourself. As you forgive yourself for your ignorance and lack of knowledge, and forgive everybody else in the same instant, at that moment, you are moving into enlightenment. Not only do you say, "I forgive you," but you also forgive as a process of being.

Your attitude is one where you would reach down into the muck and mire of where someone is and gently lift them out and cleanse them from what they had on them, as bad and terrible as it may be. That reaching into the muck and the mire to meet somebody where they are, and to pull them back out into the Light, will look like you've gone into darkness. The one you pull out, who has that junk all over them, will look at your hand and think you're as junky as they are. But as they clean themselves

up, they will see that you've got a very clean hand of enlightenment. The enlightened person doesn't care either way, because in such a person there is no judgment present.

*I believe that unarmed truth and
unconditional love will have the
final word in reality.*

Martin Luther King Jr.

There Really is No Other Way

Unconditional loving isn't being namby-pamby or wishy-washy. It is a highly active state without judgment. It's active because, in order to hold the energy of unconditional loving, you must be present and aware. To love unconditionally, you love not because of the good someone may have done or may do for you. Your love is not based upon them; it's based upon you. Whatever they do is not going to change your love for them. It's not in their hands to change it. The only thing that changes is how you participate with them, because unconditional love is non-inflictive. I may love somebody very much and know that they don't want to hear from me. I leave them alone, and I still love them. Unconditional loving can be seen as the craziest thing.

Unconditional loving is another name for individual inner peace. If we profess unconditional love, life brings us experiences to test our peacefulness. When we are tempted to respond reactively, "Why did they do that? I hate them. I'll get even with them," at that moment, we get to choose to strike back and get involved in their animosity or to tune in to the unconditional loving that just lets them be. We can choose to continue in our direction and give them the freedom to go another way.

Once we have gained the experience of unconditional loving, we know that there really is no other way because any other way causes too much disturbance inside us and we lose our peace. There is nothing passive about this inner peace, it is active and dynamic, and it spurs us on to live our lives creatively.

And did you get what you wanted from
this life, even so?

I did.

And what did you want?

To call myself Beloved, to feel myself
Beloved on the earth.

Raymond Carver

Love What Is in Front of You

When you become the Beloved by entering into the loving that you truly are, there is no need to try to save the world. It's already been saved. What the world does need is more loving; however, your job is not to love the whole world. You need only love the world that touches you— the world that is in front of you. That may be your children, your spouse, the UPS man, the supermarket checkout clerk, or your co-workers.

It really is so simple. You love whatever is in front of you, for in truth you are the world. There is no separation. You don't have to go anywhere except reside within your own inner awareness, your own natural rhythm, and let the love that is the Beloved shine out and touch others. It doesn't matter whether they are aware of it or not. You are not doing it for your own glory but for the glory that is the Beloved. That glory needs no recognition nor does it need to be defended, for it is a loving, non-judgmental state.

You can be in this tranquil, peaceful, expansive state right now. Let go of all resistance and find rest and comfort in it. And even though the things you do in this physical world may continually misrepresent who you are, never forget for even one second that the divine spark that is God resides within you.

After all has been said and done, you'll find out that you've been walking with your own Beloved for many, many eons. And one of your great realizations will be that, at all times, everything was absolutely perfect within you.

The relationship which I have found helpful is characterized by a sort of transparency on my part, in which my real feelings are evident; by an acceptance of this other person as a separate person with value in his own right; and by a deep empathic understanding which enables me to see his private world through his eyes.

Carl Rogers

The Spiritual Law of Empathy

There are spiritual laws and there are commandments. While commandments can be broken, spiritual laws cannot be—much like the law of gravity cannot be broken. A spiritual law can never be undone or untied, it is always evolving upward, moving into the heart of God.

Such a spiritual law is empathy. As you move into empathy, there is a degree of warmth present as this law manifests itself to you. It is like the warmth of a truly loving family where each soul attunes and chimes to the sound alive in the other.

There is in empathy a sense of touch. You touch me in your sorrow. You touch me with your joy. I am aware within me of that which is in you.

In empathy there is a form of sharing where those who understand you share in your greatness and also in your despair. When empathy is present in the household, there is also participation and active involvement. I partake of your grief. I sit and I hold your hand. In other words, I enter into the sharing, fully. I eat your food and drink your water. Your family is my family now. To enter into empathy, there must be this type of participation.

In empathy there is identification. Perhaps I would have done the same thing in your place. I do not judge you nor hold you guilty. I see you with respect. I can touch to you through my warmth and loving. I can share, I can participate, and I can identify, because this me and this you reside together in the Beloved. We have just separated this oneness into the physical form to look at each other.

It is only through empathy that it is possible to step into another person's shoes without displacing that person, or forcing yourself upon them, or restricting and controlling them. In empathy no one loses their own identity—the preciousness of the soul.

Besides the noble art of getting things done, there is the noble art of leaving things undone. The wisdom of life consists in the elimination of non-essentials.

Lin Yutang

Be Comfortable With Your Self

Part of finding a place of rest in this world is to let go of the compulsion to create things. It's far better to simply observe what's already in this world. Creation is complete. And you get to enjoy it. You don't have to do something. Relax and enjoy what's present.

When you do choose to do something, do it with joy. Do it with a sense of completeness. It's preferable not to leave anything hanging out, incomplete, because it will drop into the unconscious and be a drag on your energy later on. It will most likely give you a subtle sense of discomfort when you really should be comfortable doing anything, any time, all the time, with anybody.

Being comfortable isn't a license to hurt someone—that would be out of harmony with the divine. Hurting someone would make you uncomfortable, and I suggest that you always be comfortable within yourself. That way, you will always withdraw from hurting someone. That's the law of empathy.

When you live in the presence of the Beloved, you actually live in the law of empathy, where you withhold from striking and harming another individual because that is also striking and harming you, in them.

When you see someone hurting, you may feel an impulse to go help, but that often ends up interfering. The person will often want to be left alone to handle the matter. In fact, that's the way it's done. When we do it ourselves, it cannot be taken away from us—but we do not boast about it, because that can cause discomfort.

Do yourself a great favor and find a little time each day to go inside of you to that place within you that is sacred, the place that is the Holy of Holies. There you get to transcend the barriers

of the flesh and meet the Beloved. You may still have body odor, your mind may still go in circles, and your emotions up and down, but you'll find out that those things will be running you less and less because you'll be living in the spiritual part of you that is truly your life energy and the source of your rest and comfort.

Resting Point: Ways to Restore Your Energy

He who can no longer pause to wonder and stand
rapt in awe is as good as dead; his eyes are closed.

Albert Einstein

The Pause. Learning to pause is a great tool to have up your sleeve. Its value is in bringing you consciously present. You can pause a moment in your daily routine and say, "I am present. I am here, now." Then allow yourself to be with whatever is revealed.

If you find that you are hurrying, pressuring yourself, if you have a preoccupation or worry that is robbing you of energy, or you notice that your shoulders are a little high and tense, pause. Take a breath—rest in the moment and slowly allow your shoulders to lower, and your emotions to let go.

When we take a pause, we tend to notice what is around us— the patina on a vase, the shape of an object, and even the mess on the floor may suddenly transform into a divine modern art installation.

A further refinement is to bring your attention to the pause between exhaling and inhaling. Even doing this once will give you a moment of rest and restoration.

Add richness to your day by pausing.

The beginning of love is to let those we love be perfectly themselves and not to twist them to fit our own image. Otherwise, we love only the reflection of ourselves we find in them.

Thomas Merton

Saving Grace

Empathy is a saving grace. You will, through empathy, have the freedom to stand and lovingly face the conditioning that is not only yours but is in the world. Laughter is an expression of empathy. Tears are also an expression of empathy. When you understand empathy, you move into the consciousness of "You are one with me. We are walking in each others' shoes." And it becomes a really great, great day.

The voice of empathy speaks of abiding in peace and in love. You say in empathy, "I reside in you, you reside in me. We know each other spiritually. We see each other through the mind. We feel each other through the emotions, and we touch each other through the body." When we do this, we have indeed the warmth, the touch, the sharing, the participation, and the identification that are the underlying factors of the law of empathy.

Those who misunderstand will say, "Don't you have empathy for me?" That is emotionalizing. They might say, "Have some pity on me." But the law of empathy is invoked naturally, through loving, not through manipulation.

When we look into each others' eyes we may be overwhelmed with the spiritual love that the Beloved represents, and as we reach out and touch and hug, we find that we say nice things and become one with that person. We may even become lovingly protective of the person, and in doing so we fulfill the question asked ages ago, "Am I my brother's keeper?"

Yes, we are our brother's keeper through empathy because we will not strike out against that which is hurting. We will caress what is hurting, and we will lift it because we will know it and see it for what it is and bring it into harmony with the Beloved. We will know what to do intuitively and

instinctively because the law of empathy has been placed within mankind.

The law of empathy has always been here. But now it has been revealed and manifested for our time. That means it will travel throughout this world, and you will see empathy uproot and change and bring about what is once again to become new. It will touch everything. Mineral, vegetable, and animal will be touched through the law of empathy.

For the law of empathy is a golden circle, like a ring, or a crown that represents the royalty of each individual, the highest point of a human being. And those who place this ring or crown upon their head over their forehead will be crowned heirs to the kingdom of heaven.

But the school of empathy is a very demanding school. You must go into it accepting all things, cooperating with all things, understanding all things, and being enthusiastic as you work with all things. Then as you have empathy towards all things, you will glow.

The curious paradox is that when I accept myself just as I am, then I can change.

Carl Rogers

God Pours Forth the Spirit into These Days

Believe it or not, there is something positive in the experience of having been badmouthed, or physically abused, and that is you can have empathy for others who walk in the path behind you. This is where you refuse to hurt someone because, in the spiritual law of empathy, you instinctively withdraw from hurting another human being before it can even rise in sight of you. This then is living in the Beloved.

When you are attuned to the law of empathy, it will work through all of your levels—physically, emotionally, financially, mentally, and sexually. Empathy will not even permit you to err against another human being because you will pay the price immediately. In empathy we live in the Beloved, the living love of the spiritual heart, for that is our true freedom.

In that living love, empathy comes as an involuntary action, without thought. (Sympathy has a different quality and comes as a voluntary action, for example when we say, "Oh, I feel so sorry for you.") When empathy comes forward, it moves the soul, it moves the body, it moves the mind and the emotions, and completes the action at hand— fulfilling the spiritual laws of acceptance, cooperation, understanding, and enthusiasm. For empathy is based upon these spiritual laws.

Those of you who are living these spiritual laws and learning from them and loving with them will rapidly enter into this empathy in which all things will be made known to you. For God is pouring forth the Spirit into these days that are with us now, and even though we may see starvation, floods, wars, and countries going bankrupt, we will know the law of empathy. For if we don't know starvation and we have no empathy, it will be brought to us to experience it. God bless those who can move to the law of empathy, for you sidestep the lessons that would be presented to you otherwise.

If you see good in people, you radiate a harmonious loving energy which uplifts those who are around you. If you can maintain this habit, this energy will turn into a steady flow of love.

Annamalai Swami

The Sacred Tones of Empathy

To awaken empathy, you can chant the sacred tones of empathy.

The sacred tones of empathy are these:

Ani-Hu

Hu (pronounced like hue) is an ancient name of God that goes through all levels of consciousness. Ani (pronounced ahn-eye) brings forward the quality of empathy into those levels.

Invoke the spiritual law of empathy by chanting Ani-Hu.

As you do this, know that the glory goes to the Father. The glory goes to Spirit. The glory goes to God. And in this we learn of God's empathy for mankind. We were placed here as divine attributes. Our counterpart is God in spirit, for we are God in flesh.

We do not deny the spiritual light and love coming anywhere from anyone, for that is also the consciousness of love speaking to itself. When you are in the consciousness of living love, you're in the consciousness of the law of empathy.

The most radical thing we can do in this world is be joyful.

Patch Adams

Unconditional Loving

Unconditional loving is when we sincerely ask God to tell us whether we should buy this car or that house, or marry this man or woman, or go here for dinner or there for a movie, and God says nothing. When God is allowing us to decide and to learn to make mistakes and to grow, that—to me—is unconditional loving.

Unconditional loving is the action of loving you, and what you think about me or say about me is within you—it's not my responsibility and it does not affect my loving you.

Whether or not you are being unconditional in your loving is the ultimate test of all things that come your way. The test is not about my unconditional loving towards something out there. The test is whether I can be unconditional in my loving towards me.

Many people take the mistakes in their life and then beat themselves in the head with them when they are smart enough to know that beating themselves up doesn't do anything. The faster we can get back into loving ourselves unconditionally, we will, at the same time, allow others the space of their reality. They have the space to have their experience the way they see, feel, or perceive it, and we're not going to do anything to change or impinge upon it because we truly and simply do not know what is exactly, and purposefully, best for that person.

To state the obvious, unconditional loving is loving unconditionally. But it is also more than that. It is to align your mind and emotions and your body with that loving and to move through the world with its illusions, intrigue, and the dilemmas of life, and stand in the midst of it all as an unconditional lover, loving unconditionally, regardless.

And when people strike at you, know they do so because they hurt and have lost track of their own unconditional loving for themselves. The job at hand is not to tell them, "You forgot to love yourself." They don't want to hear that. They want to know, "How do I love myself?" As you start loving yourself in their presence, you will lift them, and through your demonstration, they will learn how to lift themselves.

You never change something
by fighting the existing reality.
To change something, build
a new model that makes
the existing model obsolete.

Buckminster Fuller

A Majority of One

One man or woman with their heart full of unconditional loving is a majority, regardless of what other people are doing. Yes, we're still going to go through this life doing cruddy things and making mistakes, and that's when we will need more loving than ever before. Those moments are when you really get to experience that unconditional loving really *is* loving unconditionally, because there usually is less opportunity to practice loving when everything is going your way.

When you are loving unconditionally, you won't care what I or anyone else does. It's not that you care less, it's just that in your own inner space, where everyone lives inside of you, it is a healthy, wealthy, and happy place. I found out a long time ago that if I am out of harmony with anyone inside of me, then I am out of harmony with myself, also. If you are carrying anyone inside of you that you are judging, your thoughts and feelings about them are robbing you of your energy. Bring them into harmony through love and forgiveness, or keep them outside of your inner environment. I want my inner environment to be sacred, soft, and unconditionally loving so that I can return there often for nurturance and regeneration.

There is a philosophical idea that in order to lift the planet we must work here until the last consciousness has elevated up. I'm telling you that that idea isn't so. But what *is* so is that you must bring any person out there who's inside of you, the least one, into an unconditional loving presence within yourself, or you will not be able to lift yourself above where they are.

You do this for your own growth and upliftment, so that when you go within, you will find the loving there for that least one. There is a biblical statement that when you have done it to

the least one of these, you've done it to me. The moment when you love the least one as much as you love the greatest one is when you touch into the complete oneness of the Beloved. That's when you have vitality. That's when that loving moves in through your body, mind, emotions, and the dis-eases of life start to disappear. Then a wholeness, a wellness starts to come present inside of you and lifts you up and manifests out into the world.

Everything that irritates us about others can lead us to an understanding of ourselves.

Carl Gustav Jung

The Unconditionality of Life

The ideal of living love is to be unconditionally loving all the time, everywhere. That doesn't mean that you need to be gushy or emotional. But it does mean being unconditional regardless of any outward appearance. Your inner response from your true self, the core of your being, to any situation, is one of loving unconditionally. The true self loves itself unconditionally so it, therefore, loves all things unconditionally, because the self is all things but has been individualized into a certain form. The true self is the truth, the soul, the spirit.

We're free to create according to our levels of consciousness and we can create unity; we can also create separation. We are always responsible for our creations. I know from personal experience that to be loving is one of the best things to create because I feel so much happier and joyful when I do it. That's why I tell people, "Be loving," because I know that they're going to feel better if they do it. When people are being loving, unconditionality can start taking place because if that loving is unconditioned, it means that it's not material, emotional, or mental. It is God in the unconditioned state or the Spirit. In that Spirit there's no judgment, because it's not conditioned. We call it the Beloved.

When you attune to the Beloved, you find out that you want to produce unconditional loving and be in that energy field. Those people who are also working in the unconditional energy field start blending together with it. However, if you start to produce unconditional loving with the idea of getting somebody to blend with it, it won't work. That's manipulation and you won't like the consequences. It really has to come from the place of un-condition—no condition. It's the attitude that

however the wind blows is fine with you. And if it doesn't blow, that's equally fine. That's getting into unconditionality. It can be a scary place to be when you are used to being controlling, demanding, and spoiled. But regardless, it is the un-conditionality of life that must be lived.

Whatever you are doing, love yourself for doing it. Whatever you are feeling, love yourself for feeling it.

Thaddeus Golas

When You Don't Know What Is Going On

Loving unconditionally does not mean that you have to participate with someone in what they are doing. That is their expression and their opportunity to learn, not necessarily yours. Loving unconditionally means that you accept their action without judgment and without negative reaction.

Love is the key—total, unconditional love. Even when you don't feel like loving, you love the feeling of not feeling like loving. There is no way you can separate yourself from love and maintain freedom; the only way to true freedom is to love it all.

Love yourself even when you don't know what is going on. Love yourself for being "hard-headed." Love yourself for not being able to play a guitar and sing and write music. Love yourself for being a "good-for-nothing"—you're such a lovely one. You can be everything you want to be as soon as you unconditionally become unconditional.

If you want the spiritual flow to work unconditionally, then you must let it flow unconditionally. No modifications. No conditions. No deals. Just keep it open. If you move from a state of tension, you will be blocked. If you always move from your center of relaxation, you will be free.

If your daily life seems poor, do not blame it; blame yourself, tell yourself that you are not poet enough to call forth its riches.

Rainer Maria Rilke

Are We Made in God's Image?

We must unconditionally love ourselves. If you get upset and you've lost your temper, love yourself anyway. If somebody damages your car in an accident, love them anyway. Why? Because the materialistic things of the world can be replaced and repaired, but this love that is the Soul giving forward of its divine nature is by far the Pearl of Great Price. When you are loving unconditionally, and the body is steady, the emotions still, and the mind naturally quiet, your consciousness will rise to the next level. It's automatic. We are designed to progress in an upward state, continually.

I am often asked what God's image is and what it means to be made in God's image. God's image is the expression and manifestation of unconditional loving in every shape, form, and frequency. To be made in this image is simply an indication of the potential of each and every one of us.

Whether or not we are living up to that potential can be simply evaluated on the basis of our action and reaction to outer events. If we are caught up in our ego and emotional reaction patterns, we are clearly ignoring our divine heritage. If we are involved in unconditional loving as a living expression, we are indeed made in God's image.

No man or woman is great enough or wise enough for any of us to surrender our destiny to. The only way in which anyone can lead us is to restore to us the belief in our own guidance.

Henry Miller

The Key to a Successful Marriage

Conditioned loving is challenging. That's why I do unconditional loving because it's easy— a lazy man's way out of many of the dilemmas that confront us in day-to-day living. Unconditional loving is the easy way to enlightenment. I leave the conditioned stuff to people who have nothing to do except fight. Conditioned loving is hard.

Do you know why people are free around me? I don't have conditions on what they should be doing. They feel the freedom and want to be around me. As soon as they place a condition on what I, or anyone else, should be doing—they start to have a hard time. But if they allow others to be free in their choices, all of a sudden the conditions disappear and unconditionality appears in its place where there are no judgments, there is no againstness, there is just the free flowing of consciousness. That's why I love unconditionally.

People get married for conditional loving not for unconditional loving. They want something from each other— those are the conditions. There is a way to make this work and here is the key: get really clear on what conditions you want in your relationship and lay them out in an honest, forthright way to each other. If you both agree with the conditions, then you can both agree to participate in the marriage unconditionally within those understood conditions. If the agreement is made in honesty and integrity, at the moment of agreement, the unconditional loving will start taking place, but remember the conditions need to be set up and agreed upon first. This is the freedom of practical spirituality.

Miracles seem to rest, not so much
upon faces or voices or healing power
coming suddenly near to us from far off,
but upon our perceptions being made
finer so that for a moment our eyes can
see and our ears can hear that which is
about us always.

Willa Cather

Attuning to the Beloved

Take a moment to be comfortable with yourself and in your own individual way attune into that which is the Beloved. Attune to that sacred center within you where you know goodness dwells. Attune to that same spot where you feel you really want to live, where you can express from this center into the rest of the world calmly, peacefully, and in loving. This starts then the opening of the door into the portals of the soul. This attunement is not an intellectual process but one of just giving your attention to it and resting there in a state of being.

That place in which you rest can't really be described, yet it is very real. We get in there periodically, and the joy, the bliss, the ecstasy that can come forward from that small visit with yourself can carry you over some very rough spots.

Since we dwell primarily in the negative—the world being in a negative polarity (compared to the Soul which has a positive polarity)—we find that we have, for the most part, a greater preponderance of negative things to work through. So it is a respite to enter into the Beloved—that which is the essence of divinity within each one of us. It's like a fresh breeze that blows from heaven as we neither demand nor expect anything but simply allow ourselves, life, and each person to be as they are.

It is for your highest good to find God. It's the only real good that can come of your whole existence. For the good of your soul, the God of your soul, is in itself all things.

Pay yourself a visit. Drop the pretense of existence and go within and find the Grace of God being bestowed upon you by the Beloved. You can endure all the negative things in your life because, they're nothing anyway.

It is useless to force the rhythms of life. If I live with the anxiety to go fast, I will not live well. My addiction to speed will make me sick. The art of living is about learning how to give time to each and every thing. If I have sacrificed my life to speed, then that is impossible.

Ultimately, 'slow' means to take the time to reflect. It means to take the time to think. With calm, you arrive everywhere.

Carlo Petrini

Slow Down

It's important to relax because you can never win with resistance. You win when you approach each situation you meet by slowly expanding your energy field—reaching out to meet and encompass it.

As you take each situation as it comes, one at a time, it's very easy. As soon as you feel overwhelmed or reactive, relax, rest, and gently pull your energy field back in, strengthening it by being still. Maybe you maintain your inner stillness for a moment, or a day, or a month. You simply maintain your equilibrium, looking at the situation, thinking, "Why does it think it can outlast me? While it is in a state of change, I can be in a state of spiritual holding and fulfillment and outlast the change."

That inquiry where you observe and do nothing moves you back into your center, into Spirit and Soul. You can lose that center, that sense of oneness, when you create separation by thinking that you are better than someone else. This will dissipate the spiritual energy within you. The trees and plants do not think, "I'm better than you." That's why the spiritual energy often tends to stay more present in nature.

Relax. Don't grab. That's tension. You can't truly possess or hold on to anything anyway. All you can do is utilize what's in front of you. If you try to possess, you lose. You can't even possess your own body. But if you love yourself, if you love the Soul within, you have access to all things.

So why not go a little slower in your life? Take a little more care with everything around you. Practice a little patience, because tension and fear create the blocks that stop the flow of life through you. The antidote is really very simple, and it's been stated in one way or another in almost every sacred piece of literature that has ever been written: love God with all your

heart, with all your mind, and with all your Soul. Love God in your activities, work, and play—in everything you do. And love your neighbor as yourself—love your neighbor as God.

When you realize that God has produced all things for your upliftment, learning, and growth, you start relaxing automatically. You'll know that your neighbors aren't going to hurt you, because Spirit is sustaining them through the same God force that sustains you. You can relax towards your neighbor, knowing you're on the same side—knowing that you all reside in the Beloved.

Resting Point: Ways to Restore Your Energy

The word "listen" contains the same
letters as the word "silent."

Alfred Brendel

Silence. Your endless activity and "doing" can make you so tired that when you finally take a moment to stop, listen, and relax, you will often go to sleep out of habit.

A better choice would be to be present and alert and to listen past the inner conversations of the mind, listen past the sounds of the world, and just listen to the silence. Listen attentively to whatever comes forward out of the silence.

If things start to distract and disrupt you, bring your focus back to the silence. As many times as the silence is broken, you can refocus on listening to the silence one more time.

When you practice bringing your presence into the silence, you will experience a knowing and a wisdom that will start flowing within you. It will usually bring you to a state of peace, calm, and clarity.

Then, if something comes to mind that needs to be done, instead of rushing into it, you will know that it can be accomplished in a relaxed way without breaking your connection with the inner silence.

I know God will not give me anything I can't handle. I just wish He didn't trust me so much.

Mother Teresa

There is No Separation

It's best to let go of the idea that you are separate from your fellow humans, because holding on to that illusion can block you from the transcendent consciousness. You are an individual, of course, but not in a separate way. Yes, you are special, and unique. But since everyone is special and unique, that makes you rather ordinary. So for you to make attempts to become individual, unique, or special is a waste of time. You don't have to prove it or do anything to make it so. It is so.

You do have your own individual path to walk. However, realize that it is likely very similar to the path of another. Human beings are not so different from one another and the similarities far outweigh the differences. All life has sense and purpose to it, and all human life has very much the same sense and purpose.

You are one with all that is of God. Oneness is discovered through the mystical approach, the inner spiritual realization that transcends all the ordinary faculties of man and reaches above and beyond sensation, perception, thought, and imagination. Through the mystical approach, you move into a transcendent light and sound that is the very heart of God.

To get to reality, you bypass the dualism of the knower and the object known. You evolve in your awareness to where you know yourself as both the knower and the object simultaneously. Spiritual oneness transcends all separation on all levels. In Spirit, you do not seek outside yourself because who you are encompasses all there is. There is no lover because there is no second one to be loved. There is only one. The oneness is the Beloved.

All the principles of heaven and earth
are living inside you. Life itself is truth,
and this will never change. Everything
in heaven and earth breathes. Breath is
the thread that ties creation together.

Morihei Ueshiba

Precipitating Goodness in Your Life

When you live life knowing that you are worthy of God's presence in your life, you bring good and abundant things into your life. You are open to God's love, so love comes to you. You are aware of the joy in your life, so you manifest more joy.

Manifestation is successful only if it results in a change of consciousness. That's a little different from how most people see it. Manifestation has usually been defined as the ability to make something appear physically. But if you only take into account the materialization of a physical form, you have missed the essence of creation. When manifestation results in a change of consciousness, you no longer need to see the form in the outer world, but you move to the very essence of its fulfillment inside of you and then you truly have it. Truly having something does not mean you possess it as a form, but that it is present for you in its essence.

You don't possess your breath, nor do you possess the air around you as a form. Yes, you do need it, yet when you take a breath in, there is no longer a need because it is present within you. When you find the essence of love within you and then seek a form for it, in a person, a marriage, or a family, you are taking your mental identification, putting your energy on it, pushing it out into the world, and seeking the form that will somehow match the essence you have experienced inside of yourself. It will never match. You may get the form, but you'll never get the essence by searching for it in the form. And that's why the form will never satisfy. It can never, ever, be enough. But the essence is perfectly plentiful.

To precipitate goodness (Godness) in your life, move always to the essence. Successful manifestation is moving the

goodness from the Soul, through the intuition, and into the consciousness. Intuitive knowing is a process of Soul. It is a process of moving beyond form to the essence behind it and knowing the essence.

The essence of the Soul is abundance. Spirit is naturally abundant because it is the substance from which all things are created. There is nothing that is not Spirit. To be abundant from the Soul level does not mean having access to many things; it means having access to the essence of all things and being in communion with the one essence. When you are in that divine communion, you never feel lack. So if you want to experience true abundance, practice divine communion.

After all, computers crash, people die,
relationships fall apart. The best we can
do is breathe and reboot.

Sarah Jessica Parker

How to Handle Anything

It's not doing that makes you tired. As soon as you move on something that is on its way to being completed, the energy is made available to you. It is the going back and forth, the thinking, "Should I, or shouldn't I?" that wears you out. Only rarely does the physical body get honest-to-God tired, but it frequently gets exhausted from the mental and emotional fighting inside.

Your body is working constantly, attempting to hold everything *here and now* in time and space. Your emotions are usually caught in the past. Your mind is busily setting up the future with another situation that you're not even prepared to handle. Here is a big key; you can handle *anything* by coming back to *this* moment and taking your next breath. You do that consciously now through your breath. By affirming that you are breathing in love and you are breathing out negativity, you will find yourself coming into greater balance.

The challenge for you on this planet is simple: do not ask, do not want, do not desire out of lack—because by doing that, you are doubting the existence of God, who can grow the trees and the flowers and who can certainly take care of you. If you simply affirm God's existence, saying, "I am open; I am receiving," you will find that greater things will come to you. If you can go further by saying, "Thank you, Beloved" or "Baruch Bashan (the blessings already are)," you will be awakening to even greater blessings of Spirit.

When I saw others straining toward God,
I did not understand it, for though I may
have had him less than they did,
there was no one blocking the way
between him and me, and I could reach
his heart easily. It is up to him, after all,
to have us; our part consists of almost
solely in letting him grasp us.

Rainer Maria Rilke

A Golden Moment of Eternity

It is actually easy to go through life not desiring. All you do is function on the level of your immediate need. *Immediate need.* As soon as you go on to tomorrow's need, you're in a want pattern. And as soon as you go to next month's need, you're getting into a desire pattern. Desire for the future, or memory of the past, aren't what the heart wants. The heart wants a *now* fulfillment.

You can get a headache thinking about what's going to happen in a few minutes. Yet when you forget that and live now, your headache leaves. It's amazing how fast headaches and aches and pains in the body can drop away when you live in *this* moment.

I know it can be difficult to hold steady to the moment because you're always looking forward into the next week, the next month or the next year to receive your salvation and your spiritual enlightenment. If you are always looking forward, it will always be next week, next month, next year. It will never be *now*. Come to *right now*, and you can have all things *right now*.

You may be realizing that one key to inner awareness is to *do it now*. If you use that key, you'll find that you're not rushing out into aimless activities in the world. Sometimes, when you've been projecting yourself too much into the world and the aimless activity stops, you almost go crazy because you think there's nothing to do. All you really and truly have to do is continue breathing. For the truth is that with each breath you take, God is saying to you, "I'm right here. Everything is fine." That is the eternal essence of God that is entirely present at every moment.

As soon as you declare that there is distance or there is time, that is precisely what you have to work through. The

consciousness of *now* has no time or space. It just *is*. Each moment is a golden moment of eternity. Each moment. Your next breath is your most important breath. Take it. If you didn't, you wouldn't be here. That's really living now. Each breath lifts you to a new level. From that new level, as you watch your next breath, you can slip away from everything extraneous to you. Then it becomes so joyful to take that next breath. You realize that the breath keeps the body going so that the Soul can reside in this temple and express on this level to all other manifestations of the Beloved.

Resting Point: Ways to Restore Your Energy

There are times when in order to keep ourselves in existence at all, we simply have to sit back for a while and do nothing. And for a man who has let himself be drawn completely out of himself by his activity, nothing is more difficult than to sit still and rest, doing nothing at all. The very act of resting is the hardest and most courageous act he can perform.

Thomas Merton

Doing Nothing. One of the greatest ways to restore your energy is to do nothing. It can be such a difficult thing to even contemplate as most people are in a continual state of "doing" out of habit. However, "doing nothing" can be a great way to interrupt the pattern of habitual doing. If reading this brings a sense of relief or longing, then it is a sure sign that you really do need to spend some time doing nothing.

Doing nothing is not sitting mindlessly in front of the television or daydreaming—you do enough of that already—those "activities" do not bring you a state of rest and restoration. Doing nothing is more akin to entering a state of observation, where you perceive things clearly just for what they are. From that state of observation, you have nothing to gain or lose one way or another. Because you are doing nothing, you are not involved.

An analogy is watching boats going out to sea. You observe them as they pass you. Then you observe the next one. If you

gawk, think about how you would like to be in a boat, etc., you have moved out of observation.

Observation is only about what is, not what you know or don't know about a situation. The power that comes from that, internally, is tremendous. It's an active place of neutrality. And it becomes so nice that you just want to stay in that place. You reach a state of contentment. The state of contentment allows the soul energy to activate through. The process of observing what is, is the process that releases and restores us.

Beauty is life when life unveils her holy face.
But you are life and you are the veil.
Beauty is eternity gazing at itself in a mirror.
But you are eternity and you are the mirror.

Kahlil Gibran

Awakening to the Beloved

The process of the spiritual life is, and always has been, one of continual self-awakening. As we live our lives according to the Light, love, and sound of God, and maintain our balance as we walk through this physical plane, we become more and more conscious of the fact that we walk with the Beloved. The Beloved is the form that we are all becoming, through our awakening and awareness.

The problems of life should never be looked upon with guilt, or with despair, but be looked upon as a factor of unawareness. The solutions to all of life's problems are found in that word "aware." Between the positive polarity of the soul and the negative polarity of the world, is the struggle between the freedom of immortal awareness and the imprisonment of mortal sleep.

When part of us cries out and strives for awareness of God consciousness, we can attain that awareness through a form of positive selfishness. Negative selfishness is when you want other people to live their life the way you want them to. However, the type of selfishness that says, "I will be loyal to my soul, and you can do the same," is indeed a wonderfully selfish way to live where each one walks in the consciousness of the Beloved.

This Beloved has been called many names—Christ, Buddha, the Inner Master, the Mystical Traveler—but in the greater truth, it is all of those things and everything else that exists in any dimension, anywhere, anytime, or any place.

Your job is simple. It is to find the quality of the Beloved within your Self. You don't need to go anywhere. You don't need to look outside of your Self. All you need do is awaken to the true Self within you, and everything is present, here and now, for you to do that.

The Beloved does not live in yesterday. The Beloved does not live in tomorrow. It only lives *now*, because that's all there is. So we always return to the *now* and to our own divine nature, where we meet the Beloved and merge into its loving.

The Beloved moves where there is no movement, and holds steady where nothing can hold steady. It clarifies where there is no clarification. It loves where there is no love. And it is joyful in the midst of despair. That consciousness is present with you now. The Beloved is the center of your being. All you need do is awaken to it.

Real change of self isn't found in
some new way to think about yourself,
but in the freedom from the need
to think about yourself at all.

Guy Finley

There Is Nothing to Seek

The Beloved is like a multi-faceted diamond. It's a presence that doesn't have an identifiable center. It really can't be pinpointed because it is everywhere. You reach into it when your loving comes to the place of being unconditional. The Beloved is difficult to identify because the mind likes to label, and the Beloved is not reached by the mind; it is reached by the spiritual heart.

It seems to be part of human nature to make something that is unseen into a form with which we can identify. For example, we make God an old, wise, bearded man who lives in the sky. When we make something into a form we immediately put conditions on it as part of that process. Anytime we have a form, we have a condition. And the nature of a condition is that it is restricted or limited. That's why we often find ourselves trapped by our own conceptualizing.

If you try to find the essence of a flower by pulling apart the petals, you'll get no closer to the flower. Yet its beauty has been destroyed. To find the essence of something we continually set up the form. The form then creates a condition, which then leads to limitation. Then we fight to free ourselves from the limitation that we ourselves have set up—which is another limitation.

We set up a form for the Beloved and we seek to have a relationship with that form. And that limits us because we are the Beloved. The Beloved is not separate from us. We hear the words, but it is not enough to be told this, we want to *know* it. However, our belief systems about our worthiness, what God is, and what the Beloved should be and what it looks like, all stand in the way of us experiencing the Beloved directly, within us. The mind and intellect seek something to identify with, yet there is nothing to seek, *no-thing to seek*, the Beloved is no-thing.

If only we were content with the joy and peace of no-thing. But we want the sensation of some-thing. And so we seek the Beloved in relationships. And the funny thing is the Beloved is actually there, in the other person. We touch into it and we fall in love, and we vow that there is nothing we won't do for that person, that we will serve them for the rest of our lives. However, along the way we forget that *our* Beloved is *the* Beloved and in that forgetfulness we no longer want to serve the personality's habits (which are getting tiresome), and listen to the stories (which we have heard before). We wonder, "When are they going to serve me?" With that thought, the personality has asserted itself once again and we end in divorce, attacking the very person we vowed to serve.

It doesn't end there. The yearning, the longing, doesn't go away. In wanting to know *why* we are here, we forget that we *are* here. Most of us are not here—we're holding onto the past or projecting into the future. The Beloved can only be found here and now. And the Beloved *is* here, present. There is nowhere you can go that it is not with you. There is nothing you can do to push it away. Your own ignorance and seeking can obscure it from your awareness, your own doubts can blind you, and your feelings of not being worthy of it can shut you off. But the Beloved doesn't go away. It waits lovingly and patiently for you to wake up from your slumber; to wipe the sleep from your eyes and see what is. And if, as soon as you wake up, you ask "Why?" or "How?" you put yourself back to sleep.

You will find as you look back upon
your life that the moments when you
have really lived are the moments you
have done things in the spirit of love.

Henry Drummund

Love Is Always the Answer

Some people say that when you're in love, you're blind—but I say to you that love sees where the eyes cannot perceive. Always be loving, even when it seems impossible.

For the Beloved resides in everyone. As you love the least one and the greatest one, equally, you are fulfilling God's commandment to love Him.

For you to want to manipulate someone or something indicates that you haven't found the spiritual place within where you exist as the Beloved. The one who has "got it" could care less about manipulating anything because they see the total picture of how everything has its timing and, is all right on schedule. So they sit back in a very relaxed state. Spirit pours through them and brings to them everything they need, and people say that they lead a charmed life. No, they lead a very relaxed life. They don't get irritated or upset by things.

It's really a nice day when you can sit by yourself and not have any problems. That's rest. You let go and a smile comes over your face knowing that you were the source of your problems, and all the people you blamed as being your problem were only reflecting to you your state of imbalance.

However, the only true rest I know is in the Soul when the Spirit comes to a steady place. I call that the rest point of eternity.

And it's also the rest of eternity.

God breathes through us so completely...
so gently we hardly feel it...
yet it is our everything.

John Coltrane

Experiencing God

You don't need to understand something that is already within you; you just have to awaken to your experience of it. Then understanding appears. The one who is asleep goes for abundance by manifesting illusion out of greed and insecurity. The one who is awakened only has to take in the next breath.

Breathe in divine energy, let it work through you, and then let it go. Just as you let your next breath go, so you can let go of your wants, cravings, desires, and tension.

In the age we are now in, the commandment is to love your neighbor as yourself, to love God with all your Soul, and to fulfill your destiny here. This physical level is the only place in all of the universes where you can do this, because here all the levels of consciousness are present and intact. The physical level is the glorious springboard into the higher heavens because you have the body, the mind, the emotions, and the imagination to hold the energy. The Soul can come down through it all, jump off, and throw everything up into God.

The Soul can fully understand, from this level, the totality of God. But it does not understand God physically, emotionally, mentally, or imaginatively, even though those are aspects of the body of God. As much as you can imagine God, you miss it. As much as you can feel God, you miss it. And as much as you can think about God, you miss it. But as soon as you turn into your own breath, and beyond to that which activates your breath, you can once again experience God.

And the Lord God formed man of the dust of the ground, and breathed into his nostrils the breath of life; and man became a living soul.

Genesis 2:7

Your Next Breath Is the Spirit

To know more about yourself as a spiritual being, do spiritual exercises. Then live your life as closely as you can to the preferences you select, and this will allow Spirit to come through even more.

If you live your life in contradiction to the way you prefer, the emotions and the Spirit get mixed up. Then you are thrown back and forth, and you get confusion and doubts. So choose your preference, and then move on that.

Spiritual exercises are a time to focus your attention on the higher realms of Spirit, thus putting this world into perspective. As you do spiritual exercises, you are able to gather energy from Spirit and bring it back to this physical level.

You can live without food for a long period of time, and you can live without water for a while. But you die without your next breath, and the next breath is the Spirit.

When you breathe in, Spirit comes into you. That's why it is often valuable to begin spiritual exercises by focusing on your breathing. Bring the breathing under conscious control for a little while. Breathe deeply. Envision the Light of Spirit and of God coming into your body with each breath. Take the time to consciously move your breath—and, with it, the Spirit—through your body. This can bring great relaxation, renewal, and healing.

*An old Rabbi once asked his pupils how
they could tell when night had ended
and the day had begun.*

*"When you can see an animal in the
distance and tell whether it's a sheep or
a dog?" said one of the students.*

*"When you can look at a tree in the
distance and tell whether it's a fig tree
or a peach tree?" said another.*

*"No," answered the Rabbi. "It is when
you can look on the face of any man or
woman and see that it is your sister or
brother. Because if you cannot see this,
it is still night."*

Hasidic tale

The Beloved in Everyone

Look for the Beloved in everyone. It's there behind the veil of the personality. Imagine the joy you're going to have in finding the Beloved walking down the street or at work. Since we don't know who we're going to meet, we could meet a spiritual master anywhere, any time!

Lest we become self-righteous and we miss the opportunity to see the glory of God in the human form, let's be humble, put aside our ego and personality, and let the Beloved walk in us. We don't have to talk about it, for in this process we are giving forth the Grace of God through our own being, and we will attract unto us what is ours.

Grace is given by God, and when we receive that, we become full. When we go into our heart where the Beloved dwells, then we not only have the Grace and we're full, but we're great and we're full. The heart does not say "I." The heart does not speak. The heart gives out and manifests the loving nature.

All nature, all things, all plants, all animals have a loving quality to them. Humans have the greatest loving quality because they can worship God in the intellect, in the reasoning, and in the heart. Other beings worship God at an instinctive level. Sure, they know of God. But only man can fathom the greatness, but not in the mind or in the emotions as they are too unstable and are like a roller coaster that tilts and twists.

The loving heart, the spiritual heart, is the place to be. When that is unlocked and is unfolding, if it pats you on the back or kisses you on the forehead, then you should thank God from your very being that it happened, because the loving nature is the key to all things.

For a long time it had seemed to me that life was about to begin—real life. But there was always some obstacle in the way. Something to be got through first, some unfinished business, time still to be served, a debt to be paid. Then life would begin. At last it dawned on me that these obstacles were my life.

Fr. Alfred D'Souza

Put Aside Your Conditions

One day you will arrive at the knowing that you have been walking with the Beloved. You always have and you always will because the soul is the Beloved. And the one who is self-aware is the manifestation of the Beloved. This is your birthright. You have a right to reach into yourself and find the God of your heart and a right to let others do the same thing.

The loving heart comes from God, from the Beloved. No one can create love. Love is. When it shows up, we drop everything and go with it because it never leads us astray or into lust, greed, or vanity. It doesn't abuse or take advantage of others, it leads to God. Love is the bliss consciousness in the heart. It brings health and vitality. It brings the opportunity to have all things. But since you already sit in the center of all things, why have anything else?

When we bypass the level of the personality and move into the intent of the heart, we move into loving, and a great oneness appears in our consciousness. This oneness we have called the Beloved.

Often people say, "Can you tell us more about who this Beloved is?" If their philosophical orientation is Buddhist, then the Beloved is Buddha, and if is Christian, then the Beloved is Jesus. But in my consciousness, the Beloved is God and if God is called It of Itself, this is the one I am referring to.

God is the Beloved and resides in the eternal now, unconditionally. Unconditionally means there are no conditions. If you try to condition God energy through meditating practices, breathing certain ways, or practicing spiritual exercises, doing them with the intent of conditioning God energy, then you won't even get to knock at the door for there won't be a doorway present for you.

But if you put aside your conditions and do your breathing, your meditation, your spiritual exercises with the loving attitude of, "I sit and I wait for the Grace of God, the Beloved, to touch to me and awaken me," then that is more than enough for the doorway to present itself and open towards you.

Many years later, I had a chance to ask him. I said, "Come on, you were a great man, you invited your jailers to your inauguration, you put your pressures on the government. But tell me the truth. Weren't you really angry all over again?"

And he said, "Yes, I was angry. And I was a little afraid. After all I've not been free in so long. "But," he said, "when I felt that anger well up inside of me, I realized that if I hated them after I got outside that gate, then they would still have me." And he smiled and said, "I wanted to be free so I let it go."

It was an astonishing moment in my life. It changed me.

Bill Clinton (on Nelson Mandela)

A Healing Meditation

Bring your attention to your breath and allow yourself to let go. Through your breathing, release any futility. Release any dilemma you may have. Release the pressure of seeking for something outside of yourself. Release any worry or concern.

Allow yourself to be in the presence of the Beloved. Assume you are there, even though you may not feel anything. Allow yourself to receive the unconditional loving of the Beloved into you. This unconditional loving is endless, infinite. This is the Beloved singing its own song.

This unconditional loving can't be found by searching, because it is already here, entirely present. Through your breathing, release any pressure around the heart and the back.

Realize that no one is forsaken. The Beloved is here with you in this moment. Release your concerns of what you have done or not done. Open, receive, and listen to the Beloved singing inside of you.

The Beloved sings its song right in the center of your chest where the spiritual heart resides. Feel that center expand with loving. As it expands, you find that you are standing in your own heart. And you may also be aware of a reality above your own physical body. This is the gathering in the Upper Room. For it has been said, "Where the Souls gather in my name, there I am also."

Do not be concerned about anyone around you, but lift in your loving heart, and there we will all meet as one. And we will be known by this sacred word and presence, the Beloved. In this Beloved, we see all who are the Beloved. Just relax and rest in that presence now.

Let your living love minister to you. Let it minister to all. This becomes, then, the song of the Beloved. Practice this healing meditation often. It lifts even the most despairing consciousness.

The sound of a great name dies like an echo;
the splendor of fame fades into nothing; but
the grace of a fine spirit pervades the places
through which it has passed.

James Thurber

Without Forcing Anything

Many years ago, I was listening to the Lord's prayer and I heard the words, "Thy kingdom come, Thy will be done," in a different way. I thought "Thy kingdom come" is the opening door, and all we need do is allow instead of forcing it to do something. And in that moment of receiving, we can reside in the Grace that it is coming our way.

To me that was a most dynamic moment of salvation (which means awakening and awareness). I realized, I don't have to do anything except let it come—let myself awaken, let myself become aware, and let myself exist without forcing anything. "Wow!"

I felt so joyful in that awareness that I then thought, "What do I do with this joy?" The answer I received from within was, "the same as what you do with 'Thy kingdom come',—you leave it alone and enjoy the joy!"

I then heard, "Grace is sufficient unto you." Another wow! I thought, "what about all the turmoil I'm in? If you can remove it Beloved, remove it." I heard again inside of me, "My Grace is sufficient unto you." I realized that as long as I'm being given Grace I don't need to have anything removed, because the Grace is far greater than what I've got. I was focusing upon my lack and was corrupting the goodness present. I let go and said, "Lord, I receive." And Grace was indeed sufficient unto me and has been ever since.

I am a kind of paranoiac in reverse.
I suspect people of plotting to make me happy.

J. D. Salinger

The Process of Becoming Aware

If you haven't found that divine spark of awareness, the Beloved within you, there's no need to condition how people must approach you, or what they must do to you or for you, because your way has not manifested the divine nature. There's no divine communion taking place. Divine communion is not a religious, structured approach; it is an ongoing, immediate, and spontaneous process of the "hereness" of God. The communion is the breathing in and breathing out of that divine presence that is always with you. The immediacy of it is glorious. Even in the midst of great sickness, agony or pain, you have the joy of the presence of the Beloved.

It has nothing to do with what you know or what you think or how many years you have been doing yoga or studying esoteric teachings. That's your ego parading. So what? Who cares what you've studied. Being in divine communion with the Beloved has nothing to do with what you have done or accomplished, it only has to do with now—the immediacy of this moment, here and now, and the giving up of everything that is not that. It is a pure state. As that purity establishes itself within you, and you are in communion with it, you can reside in a state of complete clarity wherever you are and wherever your inner awareness takes you.

It is a process of becoming aware for which there is no direct methodology, or chanting of a word or mantra. Those are states of preparation, not awareness. The Bible says to wait upon the Lord, which is another state of preparation.

We don't focus upon our anxiety; we have no need to create more stress. Instead we live the good life, which is being joyful and loving, regardless of what anyone else is doing, or how much money they are making, or how they are getting

ahead. That "regardless," without conditions, is the divine communion with the Beloved.

We then find ourselves patient, loving spontaneously and unconditionally, which is letting God. We find ourselves in a relaxed state, which is letting go. When we are letting go and letting God, God is the dissolver of our karma, our disturbance, our tension, and we step blissfully into the formless.

Resting Point: Ways to Restore Your Energy

To the mind that is still,
the whole universe surrenders.

Lao Tzu

Resting in yourself—Meditation. When you haven't developed an intimate relationship with life, with yourself, you'll tend to look toward having sex or acquiring more money, or to any attractive distraction to fill the emptiness inside. To fill yourself, you have to be prepared to spend time alone. This is quality time with yourself, not with a good book, not watching television, not with art, not with music. Although those have their place, learn to be quiet with your own inner self and see what you reveal to yourself.

There are many ways to meditate. There are many techniques. To this day people still think that it involves sitting cross-legged in a lotus posture. The fact is that you can meditate at any time, in any place, and it is a wonderful way to clear your mind and get a fresh perspective on life.

Any time you can bring your focus onto one thing—a flower, a sacred word, a scene in nature—you are meditating. The simplest way to meditate is to observe the rising and falling of your breath. The key with meditation is to calm your emotions and, as best as you can, still your mind. Your body can be at rest or moving—a rhythmic movement such as walking is good if you are just starting out.

Inner stillness, listening, conscious breathing—these are all meditative qualities.

That awesome Beauty gives us everything.

Whose fault is it if we go away empty-handed?

Rumi

When Grace Is Sufficient Unto You

It's so easy to take the bait the world offers us. Getting caught again in the greed for more than we need—the money, food, or sex. Once again allowing our compulsions to rule the day.

It's a relief to know that you don't have to do negative things towards your consciousness. If you overeat, over-drink, or oversleep, you can neutrally say, "Well, today I ate more than usual. Today I drank more than usual. Today I slept more than usual. Life is like that." And then get up and go on about your business. Then you can neutrally say, "And today I went on about my business. I didn't eat all day. I didn't drink all day."

The key is not to declare something right or wrong. They're equal, and in that equality they balance out.

If you look in the mirror and see yourself putting on weight, stop doing that and run around the block. Then come back and look in the mirror. You can do simple things to bring balance and harmony to yourself. Use your smarts for you, instead of using them to judge your compulsiveness, and thus become your own enemy. Judgment is not being in divine communion. In judgment you're out of harmony with your being. You don't have to put yourself down. There are many other choices.

The Beloved is always available to you. You can be free by simply not entering into the negative conditioning that you have set up. You can be free by entering into the unconditional loving of divine communion, loving God in all things around you. The marvelous thing is that God will form, as you prepare the place. And Grace is then sufficient unto you.

I have as much authority as the Pope.
I just don't have as many people who
believe it.

George Carlin

Freedom from Turmoil

There is no question that it is difficult to break free of our conditioned patterns. It undoubtedly takes a lot of attention and awareness. But I want you to consider the possibility, and open yourself to the idea, that you can be free from the conditioned patterns that throw you into turmoil.

Free doesn't mean you don't have them, but it does mean you can observe them from that place that isn't in them. That place is the Beloved.

The Beloved will go everywhere with us and will stand with us.

In this world of change,
nothing which comes stays,
and nothing which goes is lost.

Anne Sophie Swetchine

Always With You

When you let go of any experiences you have had in the past, when you release your concern about what your experiences might be in the future, when you give up your idealizations of what your relationship with the Beloved will be, and when you just allow whatever *is* to be absolutely perfect for you, then you will find the Beloved within you even closer than your next breath, and the awareness of that presence will fill you to overflowing.

You are never separate from the Beloved. It is present with you when you are up and feeling wonderful, and it is also present with you when you are down and feeling abandoned, unloved, and miserable. It is with you in your next breath.

The Spirit comes in on your breath. It is that close—or closer. Even if you would try to deny the Spirit by holding your breath, the Beloved is that which will be there when your consciousness passes out from lack of oxygen. It will function behind the consciousness and keep the breath going anyway. It will allow you to pass out, restore the breathing, and awaken you.

Death is not the greatest loss in life.
The greatest loss is what dies inside us
while we live.

Norman Cousins

Live and Die in Each Moment

The most fundamental approach to breaking any negative cycle is to come back to who you truly are and to your "own self, be true."

When you find the Self, you no longer have need for, or attachment to, any other thing. That doesn't mean you can't respond and enjoy other things, but you're not on a need level where you "die" emotionally if you don't have it. Your emotional reactions to your attachments can shut down your energy flow, and if this is maintained, disease may appear, which may lead to decay and even death.

Yet the death of old patterns is a birth into a new state of awareness and a transition point into enlightenment. There is no end to this new birth. There is always another turn in the road, another vista opening up, and another awareness coming into view. A deeper level of loving and a deeper level of commitment to the journey come present so, after a while, you don't really want there to be an end, because the journey is so much fun.

When you get far enough into your own awareness of God and Spirit and Soul, you die to this world. Your physical body doesn't die, but the old patterns of attachment do, along with the false self. Your body actually comes into its proper place, in alignment with the Spirit and the direction you are going. In that alignment, your body may become quieter and create fewer distractions that pull your focus to the outer world. This quieter place inside is a resting point, a place of renewal.

For what is it to die but to stand naked
in the wind and to melt into the sun?

And what is it to cease breathing but to free
the breath from its restless tides, that it may
rise and expand and seek God unencumbered.

Kahlil Gibran

Falling in Love with God

If we are to have deeper rest in our bodies, mind, and emotions and gain entry to the renewal found in the Beloved, we need to let go. For letting go is relaxing and letting God is simply being patient. In letting God it's helpful to know that God is formless. It's a disservice to yourself to limit God by seeking a form. Maintaining that limitation takes so much of your energy, because it goes against what is.

It's better to allow this formless Spirit of God to move through you, unconditionally, in all situations and at all times. Let it move as the wind from Heaven, of which you know neither the source nor the destination. As you open yourself to God's loving presence within you, share yourself fully with the Beloved. Hold nothing back. Be vulnerable, open, as you rest in the arms of the Beloved, for your perfect vulnerability will be your perfect protection.

Spiritual awakening is the process of giving up all forms and conditions that hold you to the material world. Let them go as you do when you breathe. With every new breath, you give up the old breath you took a moment ago. So with this new breath, breathe in Spirit and life and awareness. Now let that go so you can breathe in new life, new awareness, new awakening. It's an ongoing process. It never stops as long as you are on this earth. And when you "die" to this level, you will awaken to a new level and continue in your spiritual awakening.

When you fall in love with the Beloved, you open yourself to limitless energy and your loving becomes a creative, dynamic, moving force in your life. You see that everything is perfect, and you know it to be so. Even if something goes a little haywire in your life, it's okay. You just let go of that and partake of what is immediately present for you. If something doesn't happen in

exactly the timing you expected, you let go of your concerns and just flow with the timing as it appears.

When you are secure in your knowledge of God's love for you, you know *everything* that happens is to lift you and move you closer to your own divinity. Life then becomes abundant, magical.

I found out a long time ago that what the Beloved does has always and forever been perfect. There is nothing designed to hurt or harm us. We sometimes hurt ourselves through misinformation, misinterpretations, and misuse of energy. But we do that to ourselves. You can change that now, with this breath, with a shift in your attitude, and, above all, through loving yourself unconditionally.

Resting Point: Ways to Restore Your Energy

For God gives the Spirit without limit.

John 3:34 (NIV)

Resting in the Beloved—Spiritual Exercises. Meditation is wonderful for the body, mind, and emotions. However, I teach spiritual exercises.

Spirit is active. So, if we move into the Spirit in an active state through doing spiritual exercises, we do not first have to quiet the emotions and the mind; we can just activate ourselves past their turmoil.

Some meditation techniques teach how to quiet the emotions (which is important) and quiet the mind (which is difficult and important) and from that place, move to the Soul, which is active. It's like having to go from zero to one hundred quickly. But when you move directly into the spiritual part of you, it's much easier to bypass both the mind and the emotions.

If the mind begins to wander, you bring it back by focusing on the area between the eyes, in the center of the forehead, which is called the third eye. As for the emotions, you sit back and observe them as they come up; you see how they serve or don't serve you, how they undermine or support you. From this higher state of awareness, you can alter them. It's very difficult to alter emotions while you're in them.

Although repeating a word such as "one" in a quiet relaxed place will help quiet the mind and the emotions, often resulting in less nervousness, lower blood pressure, and greater calmness, it won't help reach into Spirit. In order to activate your

Spirit and to know it's there independent of the mind and the emotions, yet integrated in them, you use words that have a spiritual frequency, that are charged with spiritual energy.

In the Movement of Spiritual Inner Awareness (MSIA), we use two words: Ani (pronounced ahn-eye) and HU (pronounced hue). They can be said slowly or rapidly, high or low. You can experiment with them until you attune to their vibration. I've seen groups chant "Ani-Hu" in unison, and it works. A person may repeat it only a couple of times and it will work, while others have to chant it 30 to 40 times before it stops sounding alien and strange. Spiritual exercises become very easy to do as we upgrade our life from addictive, habitual, obsessive behavior, into the unconditional loving of the Beloved.

As you start to do spiritual exercises, you chant the words containing the spiritual frequencies. But at some point, you have to stop chanting and start listening for the Sound, to hear where it is and what you are listening to. The Sound lets you know into what level your Soul has extended itself. It's like a marker for you.

When you're listening to the Sound Current, you stop chanting all frequencies or tones. You sit quietly and you listen. If the mind starts to take off chattering, you start chanting again. The chanting brings the mind down to a point, and then you stop chanting so you can slip past the mind. Once you slip by it in your consciousness, you'll hear your mind talking below you, and you'll realize that it's just a chatter mind—a monkey mind, always asking questions like, "Why?" So at some point we stop asking questions, and we just start being who we are spiritually—not our personality, which is the apparent reality, but the authentic one, the Spirit inside, the one that never died.

The human race needs to be re-educated into unconditional loving and thus awakened to its divine nature. If it were easy, it would already have been done. Bringing out the God-man in people is humankind's supreme adventure. We progress, we

falter, we lift, we fall—this is the spiral of spiritual evolution, each upswing a little higher, each downturn not quite as low as the one before. All we need do is lift one more time than we fall. Slowly, more and more people are refusing to let what is less than who they are run their lives. As they discover who they truly are, their lives take on new meaning, and they know from experience that love and joy are their natural and divine heritage.

*I'm astounded by people who want
to "know" the universe when it's hard
enough to find your way around Chinatown.*

Woody Allen

How to Move On

We can let go of what binds us to our past. We can let go of our bad habits and our negative conditioning. Sometimes this letting go takes place through a process of releasing, or a surgeon's knife, a major illness, a fall, a car crash, and—please get this very clear—by just saying, "It's over."

But to say it's over, as statement of faith, means you've got to act, with your body, emotions, and mind, in a way that reflects that it is over.

You can't break up with a loved one and say it's over and then hop in bed with them. You've got to take your body, walk it out the door, and take it somewhere else—so that it *is* over.

You can't say, "I'm going to quit smoking," and then buy cigarettes. You can't say, "I'm going to stop drinking," and then go sit in a bar. You can't say, "I'm going to stop throwing up my food," and then think about how far you are from the nearest bathroom when you eat.

You've got to put yourself in line with the new behavior. Do you hear deep inside what I'm saying? You can't negatively prepare the place for yourself.

Voluntary simplicity means going fewer
places in one day rather than more,
seeing less so I can see more,
doing less so I can do more,
acquiring less so I can have more.

Jon Kabat-Zinn

So Many Wonderful Things to Do, So Little Time

We are inundated with information and possibilities. There are the yoga classes, the Pilates classes, the parties, friendships, Internet, video games, DVDs, movies, it goes on and on—and it's all within our daily reach. And then there is our vacation, the relationship with our spouse, and, oh yes, the kids need to get to school and back, to piano lessons, soccer, and karate or ballet lessons.

It's all so wonderful until we feel overwhelmed and trapped in a prison of our own making. And then the emptiness appears. That emptiness is the result of not making time for what we know in our hearts to be the most important thing.

Can you not spend a little quiet time with the Beloved?

Life has no other discipline to impose,
if we would but realize it, than to accept
life unquestioningly. Everything we shut
our eyes to everything we run away from,
everything we deny, denigrate, or despise,
serves to defeat us in the end. What seems
nasty, painful, evil, can become a source
of beauty, joy, and strength, if faced with
an open mind. Every moment is a golden
one for him who has the vision to
recognize it as such.

Henry Miller

Always Start With Acceptance

Acceptance is one of the primary laws of Spirit and one of the most vital keys to spiritual unfoldment.

There are two key approaches to working with acceptance. One is to move to the impersonal level inside you, where you are neutral and unattached, seeing the bigger cosmic picture where everything is in its right and proper place. Here you can experience life more clearly and thus accept everything that is going on.

The other approach is on the personal level. Here you select what you wish to bring into your life to enrich it, to shape your values, and to support your true quest of spiritual awakening. In other words, you select those things that will work for your highest good and your best expression.

Once we embrace the reality that all things are Spirit and that the body, the emotions, and the mind are all Spirit manifesting differently, each doing their own nature, we do not go against the nature. We move into acceptance and allow the nature to flow, without being hung up in it, without overly identifying with it.

When you have depressions, anxieties, and frustrations, don't let yourself get confused—don't think that you're sitting anywhere less than in the presence of the Beloved.

If I were given the opportunity to
present a gift to the next generation,
it would be the ability for each
individual to laugh at himself.

Charles M. Schultz

We Can Take Pleasure in God Being Here, Now.

I see so many people forgetting the fun of life. They would rather be bored and bemoan what is going on. But God is present here, now. That is something to celebrate, to be in awe of. Allow yourself to play inside, even at times when people are being serious on the outside.

The more fun you have, the more detached you can be from the circumstances of your life. You cease to be obsessed by money, by how you look, by how you compare with others, by your need for approval. You can still have fun in the midst of it all.

The greatest fun is to love what you are doing. When you truly love it, there is a pleasure and blissfulness that comes over you that lets you know that the Beloved is present. Let that presence be the center of your strength and authority. Take pleasure in all you do. You already know how to do pain, suffering, and loneliness. Wake up, the Beloved is present! That's plenty enough reason to have fun and take enormous pleasure in this moment.

On your journey back into the heart of the Beloved, all the scenery is fine. It doesn't matter what you're looking at—all of it is fantastic because you know where you are going. The world may seem haywire, you may get stuck in traffic and become late for an appointment, but you don't care because the Beloved is inside you, and you look out into the world with soft eyes, filled with love and compassion.

...don't look for me in a human shape,
I am inside your looking.

Rumi

Who Are You?

We're here on this physical plane for a short stay. Then we leave. And there are places that we will go to that are so glorious. We are heirs to the kingdom. We inherit it by divine right because of who we are.

I know it can be difficult to relate that idea with the physical disturbances that we have in our bodies, and the problems we create with relationships and finances, and the dilemma of what we are going to do with our lives.

Some people say that they have a Soul. That's approaching it backwards. It's more accurate to say that the Soul has a body. We are Soul. We are Spirit. We are the Beloved. We are divine. And we have a body to use while we awaken to that reality.

You can stop what you are doing just in this moment, to move behind your eyes to who you are.

It is so easy to identify with the body, thinking that you're your stomach that's upset, or that you're the pain in your back or in your shoulder, or even that you are your gray hair or wrinkles.

Let's just take a minute to see if we can find out who you are:

Relax the body.

Focus on your breathing, flowing in and out.

Receive your breath, then let it go.

Just allow that process for one minute.

Now, let your emotions go.

If you have an uptight feeling in your stomach or back, or anywhere, just leave it alone.

Be quiet with the body.

Be still with the emotions for one minute.

Now, calm the mind by being completely present.

No body movement.

No emotions.

No mind.

Who is doing that inside of you? Who has quieted the body? Stilled the emotions? Calmed the mind? That, my Beloved, is you. You, who are much more than body, emotions, and mind. It's the eternal you that can do that.

I know the mind starts up again and the emotional disturbances return, but now you know that is *not you*, and you can let it go so much more easily. Let the mind and emotions be out of bounds at this time.

Right now, there is only you and God, the Divine, the Beloved, the Christ, at this moment. That's all. A quiet, a calmness, a resting point.

Listen to me brother! Bring the
vision of the Beloved in your heart.

Kabir

Walking With the Beloved

It's so simple to say that if you walk with your own Beloved, all things will find harmony within their level. Yet to walk with the Beloved is, initially, a very difficult process because we must walk in loving neutrality.

For many, the Beloved is a nebulous concept because it is everything they have wanted, wished, and prayed for—yet they are still waiting for it. At the same time, there is no waiting because the Beloved does not exist in a waiting period; it exists right now. We get a glimpse of what that is, in a sense of peacefulness and calmness. It can also be that in the midst of our tension, our tribulations, and our fears, we find the Beloved is walking with us through it all.

Before we can know the Light, we must partake of the dark. And in the depth of darkness, there is great light. Many people fear darkness because it has traditionally contained black magic and evil, terrible things. Yet, these are all just interpretations of the consciousness, the conditioning, and the personality of the beholder. The things we call witchcraft, black magic, and the occult arts are still just a part of that thing that is the Beloved, manifesting in many diverse ways. Sure, it is the negative side of things, but it is unwise to get negative about negativity. The only thing I have found to work is loving. When that loving becomes unconditional, which is a neutral state, we are in the Beloved. There is no judgment, no strain, and no tension. It's a beautiful state to be in.

So whenever someone wants to bend your ear with gossip and talk of upset and dread, don't listen to them. It doesn't matter that they feel what they're saying is right or that they must save you from yourself. No one can save you from yourself. You are yourself. You are the Beloved that walks eternally.

Put love first. Entertain thoughts that give life. And when a thought or resentment, or hurt, or fear comes your way, have another thought that is more powerful—a thought that is love.

Mary Manin Morrissey

Growing into the Beloved

How do we become more and more aware of the Beloved? We become more aware by growing spiritually. How do we grow spiritually?

We grow physically by taking food, water, and air into our bodies.

We grow emotionally when we receive love and support and encouragement, particularly when times are tough. For example, when someone says lovingly to us, "Come on, stand up. I know you can do it." And we do indeed stand up and, by doing so, grow and mature.

We grow mentally by becoming educated and incorporating that education into our personality, and by taking in information and learning and memorizing it.

So it is by taking that we grow physically, emotionally, and mentally. However, it is through *giving* that we grow spiritually.

We *give* mentally by sharing what we've learned with others. We *give* emotionally by loving and supporting people. We *give* physically by being of service and helping others.

Above all, we give our loving. There is something transcendental in the process of giving love.

Through this giving, we grow spiritually and become aware that there is one Beloved in ourselves and in others.

The aim of life is to live, and to live means to be aware, joyously, drunkenly, serenely, divinely aware.

Henry Miller

You Love Everything Present, No Exceptions.

You can never find the Beloved until you reach into spiritual consciousness. Then, lo and behold, you see the Beloved everywhere you go. And though you have great love for humanity, you do not try to possess or control any one person, because it is the spiritual quality you are loving.

Although the corporal form is always going to change, fall away, and decay, the Beloved sees past that, and assists us to step across the threshold of the flesh and enter into the reality that we all are. That reality is love, peace, and joy. And the living of it is to enter into the Beloved.

Living love means that your love extends unconditionally to all things. You love everything present, no exceptions. Then the whole spectrum of your life takes place within the Beloved.

Anyone who is residing in the power of loving is never destroyed, never separated, and is always free, always up, and always growing.

And as you relax and merge into the presence of the Beloved, you will be able to look past the inadequacies of the body, mind, and emotions and see the Beloved present in all who come to you.

Finish each day and be done with it.
You have done what you could.
Tomorrow is a new day; begin it well and
serenely and with too high a spirit to be
encumbered with your old nonsense.

Ralph Waldo Emerson

A New Role in Life

We play so many roles in life. We play the martyr, the hero, the depressed one—it goes on and on. I want to give you a new role to play and try on for size; it's one you can play 100 percent. I am asking you to play the Beloved. You don't need to have a wide, dramatic repertoire; just be this one thing.

It is really fine with me that you play any role you want to, even if that role is a negative one, because the Beloved gives you space and freedom to play all the roles. I do suggest that you don't hurt yourself and don't hurt others. Be loving instead. When you love others and you look at them, that place inside of you that is love comes alive. And right behind that place of love is the Be-Loved-One.

The being that you are is the Being-Loved-One. Did you get that? Give yourself a moment to take it in. Love isn't enough. The Be-Loving-One is enough. Behind all the roles we play and the masks we put on is the Beloved, behind all of it.

Start by saying, "I am the Beloved." At some point that statement becomes something that rolls deep within you and you just know the reality of it. For now, just do your best to really own that you are the Beloved. Start by letting all your actions, even the mundane ones, be loving, even if only for a few minutes. Then expand the time gradually.

Let me share with you something important about this process. The closer you get to the spiritual source that is the Beloved, the more inspired you will be towards achieving the greatness that you want to do in this world. You will feel so energized towards your goal in the world, but I question your ability to maintain that energy. Because I know that as soon as you walk down one of the paths of your endeavors towards

greatness, you'll also separate yourself from the source that gave you the energy to go.

Here we have the dilemma: If you want that, you have to go and get it. If you go and get it, you lose the source of energy that propels you to go and get it. If you don't go and get it, you don't get it. What should you do?

The answer is to connect with the Beloved in whatever way works for you—affirmations, devotion, meditation, spiritual exercises, unconditional loving—and maintain the connection as you walk towards what you want. As you walk towards it, if it seems the Beloved separates from what you are doing, then go back inside and connect with it even more deeply. If it separates again, I would strongly question whether what you are doing is for the highest good.

When there is the feeling of separation, you are the one who moved. When you can have the Beloved with you in your actions, you will start transcending all the things around you. The Beloved then becomes your guiding light, second by second.

I say "The Beloved" because that seems to be it for me—there's neither a love nor a lover. There's just the oneness and in that we are all the same thing. When you have the Beloved walking with you on the path you are treading, you'll find that a world of karma has gone, just disappeared.

Suffering and joy teach us,
if we allow them, how to make
the leap of empathy, which transports
us into the soul and heart of another person.
In those transparent moments we know
other people's joys and sorrows, and we care
about their concerns as if they were our own.

Fritz Williams

The Only Grace Is Loving God

The only Grace is loving God. When you are loving God, Grace is extended back to you, in all shapes and forms. Once you know yourself and the Beloved within you, you will not strike against another human being. You will withhold the strike and keep it back, because that form of loving is once again entering into the Grace. It's not only the Grace of loving God; it's the Grace of loving each person as God incarnate.

Once you receive the Grace of loving God, that loving starts to purify you as a prince or princess of the higher consciousness. You start to once again come into the royalty, the purple majesty of your being, and negativity, in and around you, is transmuted into a higher form.

If you are loving God, and I mean really loving God by being centered and filled with that rather than being preoccupied with worldly concerns, then Grace abounds with you. And whatever you do becomes a blessing. It just turns out right. People actually rejoice that you are around.

When you are living in Grace, you release the self-centered concerns of the ego and you disregard what moves you into upset and suffering. Instead you turn to fill yourself with God's abundance, the keynote of which is loving.

There is a spirit that is independent from materiality. That spirit has often been called, among other names, the Spirit of Truth. I've often just referred to it very simply as the Beloved, because it's always been that with me. Just always that. Always. Forever and ever. When you connect with the Beloved, you walk and live in Grace.

For true love is inexhaustible; the more
you give, the more you have. And if you
go to draw at the true fountainhead,
the more water you draw, the more
abundant is its flow.

Antoine De Saint-Exupery

It's Worth the Effort

As we connect more deeply with the Beloved, we become clearer. Although invisible and intangible, paradoxically, we can somehow feel it with our subtle senses. When we are in the company of the Beloved, we're in touch with the divine, the unconditional essence that is our true self. As we maintain that connection, whatever we do is loving and becomes for the highest good. It cannot be anything else.

When we lose touch with the Beloved, what we do may be well-intentioned, but it will usually be motivated from our ego, which is another way of saying that it will have a conditional quality. Perhaps we are looking for recognition or approval.

If it were easy to let go and trust the Beloved, the multitudes would have done it. I can only tell you that it is well worth the effort.

Sometimes the path that leads us to the Beloved may need a little repair work. Maybe the bridge of our awareness has crumbled and needs to be restored. Perhaps the weeds of our accumulated things have grown across the path and need to be cut back. Maybe the obstacles of our resistance are in the way and need to be removed. Perhaps you've separated yourself with a wall or moat, and now you need to dismantle that which has appeared to defend you from the perceived outrages of the world.

Simply recognize that the walls have imprisoned you and that your allegiance to material things has been a fictional sense of security. Your true security is found in the freedom of the Soul.

You can drop everything that is not speaking truth inside of you, now, and return to the divinity that waits with infinite patience for your homecoming.

Rabbi Bunam said to his followers:
Our great transgression is not that we
commit sins—temptation is strong and
our strength is slight! No, our transgression
is that at every instant we can turn to God—
and we do not turn!

18th Century Hasidic Text

Turning to the Beloved

A prayer of high consciousness would be one where we ask, from deep within us, to turn to the Beloved, to the Christ within, the God center—to really turn to that. Yet the false self doesn't want to do it, because it dies when that action takes place. So it hangs on with its envy and emotional disturbances, masking the true self, which is our love, our compassion, our joy, our knowing, our right action, our right living, and the sharing of our spiritual love. This is what we all want. We all want to manifest our true self.

Many people are becoming aware of their true selves, their divinity. They say, simply, "I know now." Their reward is to awaken.

When we awaken ourselves in each other—I in you, you in me—we do indeed love, because the Beloved is us, and the only thing that sets us apart is the personality. This awakening is a celebration, for at long last you have stepped into who you really are.

The angels up there (and there are angels up there) sing aloud every time someone says, "I am the son of God. I am living love. I am the beginning and the end. I am all that has ever existed and that will ever exist." When you manifest this, then you also are the Light and the Way. Jesus said that these things he did you, too, will do, and even greater. How are you going to do them unless you become a son of God, unless you know divine love, human compassion, and empathy? The human being is one of the greatest glories of all creation because God resides at the center of each one.

For all that has been, thanks.

For all that will be, yes.

Dag Hammarskjold

Getting Your Energy Loose and Free

We humans don't like to think about our incompletions. So what we have not completed gets pushed down into an unconscious realm inside of us. Although that realm doesn't see, doesn't hear, and doesn't think or feel because it is asleep, it does have information and it does pull on our energy. You can feel it when it's time to do something about an area you have been avoiding or procrastinating about. As you approach that area, you will start to get tired, achy, and sometimes you will even start nodding off. That is because you are in the area that is sleeping.

This is the time for you to stay present and awake, for this is where you have been avoiding living. You have found the area inside of you that is unconscious, that's not aware, that's sleeping, and that has a large amount of your energy locked into it. Imagine getting that energy loose and free.

You can free that energy in this moment, by moving your body into action and starting the process of completing. As you start to do this, you will feel the energy coming loose and free inside of you, and you may find that all sorts of aches and pains will release.

This is a healing action, not necessarily healing in terms of disease, but certainly healing in terms of completing your life patterns and your goals. It's so extremely important because as an area inside of you that was asleep awakens, your energy stops leaking away into it and becomes immediately available to you as a conscious, awake person.

I implore you in God's name,
not to think of Him as hard to please,
but rather as generous beyond
all that you can ask or think.

Abbe De Tourville

The Key to Life in this World

You may be aware of many times in your life where you became excited about completing a project, and once you got going on it, you stopped because it seemed so overwhelming.

We drain off our energy when we say something is too much and that we can't do it.

Many people looked at the book *Gone with The Wind* and said that they couldn't read it because it had too many pages. But those who read it did so one word at a time.

That is the whole key to life in this world—the doing. The doing process is one of physically taking your body and moving and completing. You'll find you will have all the energy you need supplied to you when you work within the consciousness of completion.

Resting Point: Ways to Restore Your Energy

*When I look back on all these worries, I remember
the story of the old man who said on his deathbed
that he had had a lot of trouble in his life, most of
which had never happened.*

Winston Churchill

Don't Worry, Be Happy. Anything you are carrying around inside of you, even good memories, takes energy to hold. The energy that you are using to hold anything in the past, or anything in the future, such as anxiety or worry, is energy that is not available to you right now.

It is not necessary to worry or pressure yourself. It all works out perfectly, contrary to anyone's thought processes or how they feel about it. So I suggest that you not only love what's going on with you but that you learn to laugh about it inside of you. Laughing frees up energy.

We tend to take ourselves too seriously. That's the real worry! If you have an overweight body, you had better love it because you've got it. And if you love it, there is a good chance that some of the weight will dissipate because you've reduced the worry and the holding of energy that goes with it—where thought goes, energy follows, then it manifests. So love your new lighter body, even though right now it's a little heavier.

You can take that idea into your daily life by thinking and seeing in your mind more of what you want. Get a clear, positive image in your mind and energy will start to follow that. You can get a picture out of a magazine and paste it on your mirror in your bathroom, and everyday you see that it will be programming a place inside of you with a positive image of what you want.

You are a creator. If you can create a negative fantasy in which you lose, i.e., worry, concern, anxiety about the future, you can certainly create a positive fantasy in which, with joy, laughter, and health, you walk into the wonderful future you have envisioned.

God does not die on the day when we
cease to believe in a personal deity,
but we die on the day when our lives
cease to be illuminated by the steady
radiance, renewed daily, of a wonder
the source of which is beyond all reason.

Dag Hammarskjöld

Energy Follows Thought

Energy follows thought, and that energy will always go towards completion. So it's wise to always move towards completion; otherwise, our energy gets backed up and misdirected and will cause us to become tired, and often very ill.

The master key to completion is in our hands. We are the ones that decide when something is complete or finished, and we can declare it so. It's when we do not make the decision—when we do not choose to decide—that we can have problems with ourselves. You see, when we don't choose, a decision is still made—by default.

Because energy follows thought, my advice has always been to hold thoughts that uplift you. Hold images in your mind that you want more of. Be careful what you ask for because if you get it, you also get what goes with it—which is fine if, when it does come your way, you are prepared to handle it to completion.

The sacred scriptures all over the world have a similar message in their texts. The message is, "He wins who endures to the end." That is another way of saying, "Finish. Complete." The spiritual energy becomes available immediately when the demand for it is placed. It doesn't become available by sitting down and waiting. We must demand of the Spirit—not with our minds or with our emotions but with the physical movement of the body—in order to have the spiritual energy supplied to us. That's one of the prime reasons we have a physical body.

If you decide that you can't move until you get more energy, you'll be stationary for an awfully long time. As soon as you start moving your body, that very action says that you need more energy, and that energy will start moving into you. And if you use the energy to complete and to finish, you will be supplied more from a higher level.

In life, satisfaction is experienced when activities are brought to a state of completion. Loss of energy and loss of control are functions of incompletion. The result of completing things releases one's ability to create.

William A. Ward

Two Key Words for Our Consciousness

When you find that you don't have enough energy, you're feeling tired and you don't know why, I would start to take a look at what you've started and haven't completed. Completing what you put in motion is so important as it is part of the destiny of each human being to complete. This is why the focus of the human consciousness is one of completion.

We rarely ever start to eat thinking we're not going to finish it, or leave our home without an idea of where we are going. We seem to always have a goal out there that we're striving to reach and bring to completion.

Goodness, we start so many projects! Those projects are not only started physically, but they can also be started in our minds and in our emotions. When we begin the project, it always seems like a good idea. Then, very often, another project that we "must do" comes to mind, and then another.

All of the "I'm going to do's" that are not finished are little hooks that hang out in our unconscious level wanting energy to feed them. Those hooks then grab onto whatever comes around in our lives and pull energy away from us.

Every project we put in motion demands a level of energy. We have no choice in the matter at all. The choice was already made when we said, "I'm going to do this project, and this one, and this one." Even though some projects are more important than others, as long as they are incomplete, they lie in the unconscious, equally.

You may ask, how do you know it's there when it is unconscious? You know it indirectly. You may be having a conversation and something is mentioned in passing that you associate with something that is unfinished. This immediately

triggers a release of energy—perhaps you become flushed, or fidgety. You may find yourself being judgmental of yourself, which then drains away more of your energy.

The more projects you have going, the more thinly you spread yourself out. The key to prevent your energy from leaking away into the unconscious is very simple and entirely in your hands—you intervene, consciously. For example, if you have an unread book sitting around for months and you know you are not going to get to it, pick it up, open it, and then close it and say, "I'm finished. I'm not going to read it anymore." That's all your consciousness has to hear—"I'm finished."

After all, don't we declare the end of things anyway? "This romance is over." "This marriage is through." "This job is finished." We are the ones who declare it. Don't you think it's marvelous that this is all our own ball game, in which we're the umpire, referee, batter, catcher, pitcher, and runner?

One of the most useful things I can say to you for living in this world is if you want to have greater health and more energy, move things towards completion.

What is necessary to change a person
is to change his awareness of himself.

Abraham Maslow

Building Inner Trust

This whole world boils down to one word, *energy*. That energy is either used for you or used against you, but it is used. That's extremely exciting to know because the more you can complete in your life, the more you will have the feeling of fulfillment and accomplishment. Then you can truly rest inside of you knowing that nothing is undone. You may still have unknown or hidden incompletions, but you relax because you have built the inner trust that when they reveal themselves, they will be completed.

The best thing you can do to enhance your self-trust is to develop the habit of taking responsibility for all your creations (which is everything in your life) and completing what you start. You are the one in charge and responsible for your life, and even if you've empowered something or someone else through blame or playing the victim, you are still in charge and responsible for your life. You can't get away from it.

Changing a habit takes time and patience. So to build inner trust, relax, be gentle with yourself, and do keep your word with yourself—one small agreement at a time.

Do yourself a big favor and start now to develop the habit of completion. It is your destiny.

Most of our obstacles would melt away if,

instead of cowering before them,

we should make up our minds to

walk boldly through them.

Abraham Maslow

One of the Most Worthwhile Things You Can Do

I cannot emphasize enough that completing what you start is one of the most worthwhile things you can do for your health and well-being. It's a joyful process because, as you complete, the unconscious starts clearing, your energy is returned to you, and you begin to live in the present making conscious decisions and completing them on the spot. When the Bible says that the evil of today is enough, it is telling us not to put things off until tomorrow.

No matter how beautiful something looks in the world, no matter how it glitters or how glamorous it is, it's always going to corrupt and decay. You're the one who is going to have to maintain it and maintain it and maintain it, and that takes your energy. So make sure that it is important enough for you to put your energy into in a purposeful way, or drop it so you can go on to complete other things.

Student, tell me, what is God?

He is the breath inside the breath.

Kabir

Breathing in the Essence of Spirit

There is something about your next breath. That next breath is how close you are to Spirit. That's your source of energy right there in front of you. That's the Spirit, the energy, the Light, all of it, right there. Take that next breath as if you really were—and you really are—breathing in the essence of Spirit. Use that Spirit and that energy to sustain you in your life pattern. Use it to lift into the true self that you know is really you and into the consciousness of your own Soul and the awareness of the supreme God.

Allow yourself to enter into the process of spiritual understanding and maintain your calm by consciously and directly holding your inner focus—not letting flights of fancy lead you where they will. Come back to this moment, continually, and you'll find that tensions disappear, distractions disappear, and you enter into the resting point of right now.

For a while, this pure, centered consciousness will come and go. The negativity of the world will constantly reappear, but it is not a crisis to destroy you. Have the attitude that the negativity is a wayshower for you, pointing the direction to your next level. The higher consciousness then reappears, and you secure a new level so that you don't backslide. In that new level see things anew.

Don't try to bring along the old and despairing pattern of the previous level, otherwise you may enter into God Consciousness being so familiar with your old habit patterns that you fall out of it. Those who realize God Consciousness are those who enter into it, hold to it, and maintain it as the one thing they must never forget.

The moment one gives close attention
to anything, even a blade of grass,
it becomes a mysterious, awesome,
indescribably magnificent world in itself.

Henry Miller

The Ultimate Point of View

For a moment, allow yourself to take an ultimate point of view. There is no *bad*. Ultimately, it doesn't matter how much money you owe, who you sleep with, or how often you get drunk. Ultimately. It may matter for right now, because this is the only ultimate that you may know in the boundaries set by your physical body. But in the pure Light of God, there is no morality.

You may ask why then do so many people preach good and bad? I don't honestly know. Maybe they are on a God trip, thinking that they've got the right answer, and they want to persuade you to believe them. Perhaps they are saying that their God is better than your God.

Yet God's will for each of us is for us to know God, and everything is set up to support that. So you can see all your experiences as opportunities to take one more step towards God. And the way to know God is to love as Jesus loved—unconditionally, through all things.

With a body comes maintenance and a lot of outer rigmarole—changing clothes, changing soap, changing hairstyles. But inside we change the attitude. The key to spiritual awareness in the physical plane is to watch our attitude.

It may be that watching your attitude is the only thing you're going to get done today. But get it done.

Keep your hands open,
and all the sands of the desert
can pass through them.
Close them,
and all you can feel
is a bit of grit.

Taisen Deshimaru

The Key to Spiritual Unfoldment

Much of your ability to be open to new things, to alter your patterns of behavior, and to grow depends on your attitude toward the situations in which you find yourself. If you can keep a positive attitude, you can learn from any situation. When you continually grow and lift in consciousness and awareness, life can be a beautiful experience. If you hold to a negative attitude, your life will probably be one catastrophe after another, or at least that is the way you will perceive it.

When you are in a state of inner discontentment, it gets projected onto the world and you then stage your revolution "out there." Yet it's not changing anything. It's comforting to know that when you change your attitude, you may not have to change anything else in the world around you, because it's all being reflected from your inner environment anyway.

When you find yourself getting caught up in the ego as it expresses through a negative habit pattern, your key to freedom is in your attitude. There is no good or bad, no moral judgment in Spirit. Just watch your attitude. And if you feel concern, stop it. If you don't stop it, enjoy it. Don't attempt to isolate yourself into an attitude of, "This is the way I am and I can't change." At some point, you're going to die, and that's going to change you. So there's no need to stand against the reality of this level. Resistance patterns can stop the spiritual flow.

It is your attitude toward things that either blocks you or frees you. The key to spiritual unfoldment and, of course, development beyond the personality is to deal positively with situations. It's not hard. What's hard is the negative attitude that goes before you. The best attitude to have is where, no matter what someone may say or think about you, what's

important is what you say and think about you, because after they're gone you are still with yourself.

The big key for me was when I realized I could shift my attitude, that I was fully responsible for myself, no matter what the weather was like or what the people around me were doing. And I am still responsible for what I create for myself, moment by moment. I am also the one in control of my creation, as you are the one in control of yours.

Nothing has to be labeled "good" or "bad." It is all in your attitude; it is all in your approach.

Tell me what you brag about
and I'll tell you what you lack.

Spanish Proverb

It's All Right Here

So many people want to know why we are here. If the answer lay in the mind, the engineers would have figured it out and would be our spiritual leaders. If having power in the world was the answer, then the politicians would be our enlightened guides. If the answer is found in fame and glamour, then our celebrities would offer us much more than publicity and good looks. Our true leaders are those who look at life in a radically different way. They know that love is the radical solution. It's radical because most of us don't approach life that way. For the most part, we approach life reactively, trying to control rather than letting go.

The answer is that out of God come all things, that God loves all of its creation, and that not one Soul will be lost. This is the context for living a life without fear or worry. As you integrate these truths into yourself, you will let go and relax into the arms of the Beloved.

When we hold on to materiality, we find that the materiality is really holding us. Yet, when we relax, we open to an expansive place where anything can happen, where there are so many possibilities. Many of us are unwilling to go to that place. We want a guarantee that everything will be okay, that we'll have enough money for the rest of our lives. Since that approach is not the place of openness or spontaneity in which the Spirit resides, we automatically withdraw from the immediacy and intimacy of life. We freeze and become tense. We move into resistance and thus we build our prison and live in lack.

The lack then draws our attention out into the world where the eyes are always hungry. The antidote for lack is gratitude. Gratitude is a choice, an attitude, an approach towards life. My gratitude for this moment does not depend on what is going on

in this moment; it is the moment, regardless of what is going on, that I am grateful for. My gratitude for this breath is not about the breath. It's that I am breathing, that I recognize it comes from a higher source, and that I am alive. Gratitude is a moment-to-moment celebration.

He made man, and put his heart in the midst of the body, and gave him breath, life, and understanding.

Ezra 16:61

This Constant Awakening

We could say that your breath is a truth. You don't have to interpret it and it isn't based on your thoughts or feelings. Whatever is going on in your life, you breathe in and out. Sometimes you breathe quickly, sometimes slowly, but you are always breathing, until your time here is done. At that point, your breath isn't a present truth; something else will be truth for you.

Holding on to anything, whether it's an inner revelation or your own breath, is futile. You can't even hold on to your physical form, for every body is in the process of aging, regardless of what steps you take to deter the process. Nor can you hold on to someone else. You may wish to possess their mind, body, or emotions, but that, too, is a limited game.

Some people say, "I love you," to express the overflow of divine energy. Others say, "I love you," in an effort to hold on to a particular relationship. People may use emotional persuasion to keep a relationship going: "I need you." "Don't leave me." "Tell me you love me." If words and emotions did it, there wouldn't be separation or divorce. There is clearly more required to keep a relationship going than words and emotions.

What, then, keeps a loving relationship together? The same thing that creates spontaneous spiritual understanding: an awakening to the inner truth that already is. And it's not just one awakening. It is a constant awakening. You understand, and you express this understanding within yourself and in relationship to others, and you continue your process of spiritual inner awareness.

We must have the stubbornness to
accept our gladness in the ruthless
furnace of this world. To make injustice
the only measure of our attention is to
praise the Devil. If the locomotive of
the Lord runs us down, we should give
thanks that the end had magnitude.
We must admit there will be music
despite everything.

Jack Gilbert

The Value of Being Here

"This too shall pass." It always has. It always will. So why place yourself against the flow of your own divine nature through tension and concern? I know you don't want anything to upset you, but that is not what this level is about. This level gets disturbed; change is what it's about. The emotions get disturbed. The mind gets disturbed. The Soul is not disturbed, however, but it often disturbs to let you know that it is there, beyond the disturbance.

Just before dawn comes the darkest time. And we are, all of us, sitting right on the edge of the great Light. But we could sit on the edge of that for an eternity. And that is okay with the Beloved. The Beloved is not uncompassionate, it's just okay with what's going on.

We are dwelling in one soul. We are all that one soul. We are all here on this planet, playing a role, involved in this great game of awareness. But we neglect learning. We neglect experimenting. We neglect being. We neglect doing. We neglect to fully involve ourselves in that which will work. We'd rather daydream or stay in our wishful thinking. For some strange reason, we'd rather castigate ourselves according to someone else's belief system, and it is all going to change eventually anyway.

If it were easy to do, you would already have done it. I know this. But then you came here because you saw that you could learn more, in a third dimensional body, than anywhere else and in the most effective way possible. That is the immense value of being on this earth. The Soul does not care if it's illegitimate, poor, black or white, with one leg, no teeth, or bald, as long as it can be in a body and learn. We learn faster here, much faster than anywhere else.

*In the attitude of silence the soul finds
the path in a clearer light, and what is
elusive and deceptive resolves itself
into crystal clearness.*

Mahatma Gandhi

The Silence That Roars

When you share in the silence with someone, you can just be together, saying nothing, and yet be communicating on a higher level. This is when we say the silence was golden, for indeed it does have a golden quality.

So many people think that if they are with someone and there is no talking, then something's wrong. But to sit and hold in the silence can unveil to you so many inner riches. In the simple, receptive act of being silent and listening, so much can be received. However, many people when they reach that inner place, instead of going deeper, they go to sleep. Their habit pattern is to sleep when their mind becomes quiet and they listen within. It is much more satisfying to be alert, awake, and listening. You can always sleep later.

Next time you are waiting somewhere, for a bus or train, in a doctor's office, take time to listen to the silence. This is difficult, because your mind will think it's ridiculous and a waste of time, and you will start to get into a conversation with yourself. Instead of that nonsense, step into silence. If you get distracted, then bring yourself back into the silence again.

When in the silence, an intuitive knowing starts to awaken. When the wisdom within you starts to open up, you may start thinking about what is being revealed. Thinking shuts off the flow. It's better to just listen. You may think that you had better write the revelation down before you forget it. How can you forget what comes to you from your Soul? It is truth. There is nothing to do with truth, just be that.

Take time now to be in the silence. Become quiet. See how long you can be in communion with the silence. As you drink of this sacred moment, receive guidance from your Soul, from the Spirit.

Oh, they loved dearly:

their souls kissed,

they kissed with their eyes,

they were both but one single kiss.

Heinrich Heine

Awakened by a Spiritual Kiss

In Shakespeare's *Julius Caesar*, Brutus says to his friend Cassius upon going into battle, "If we do meet again, why we shall smile;

If not, why then, this parting was well made."

I've often reflected on those beautiful words. No matter how we leave people, whether on a journey or in what we call death, let's make it a "well made" parting, where we part without remorse but with joy and love and perhaps a tear in the eye. In that joy we bring whomever we are leaving into right now, and we never miss them. We always have them in the loving consciousness within us. We have the inner fulfillment without the tugging, theirs or ours. And we are okay missing them because we have the fullness inside—there is no lack. In this way we walk with the Beloved, the spiritual consciousness that we all are.

We've all been through many existences, mostly in a dreamlike state unaware of that slumber until we are awakened by the spiritual kiss of the Beloved that awakens us to who we really are. And then we ride off, we might say, with the hero, the Prince Charming, the Spiritual One into the great castle of the Soul. And we reside there forever.

It's not just a fairy tale; it is a great truth and reality. We are awakened to forever walk arm and arm with the Beloved. We walk with our Beloved within. If we walk with the Beloved in this outer physical world, we can become discouraged because we are looking for something perfect that is in our minds. That's why the Beloved does not walk with you physically, because it's too easy to become disenchanted on the physical realm. The Beloved always walks with you spiritually.

*I long to accomplish a great and
noble task; but it is my chief duty
to accomplish small tasks as if they
were great and noble.*

Hellen Keller

Sealing Our Energy Leaks

When we are operating out of our habitual responses, we are not consciously present. We walk around thinking we're alive and human, but we're in a zombie state, unconsciously eating, smoking, procrastinating on what needs to be done, or whatever.

Our habitual patterns, and the defenses we put up to protect them, pull on our energy, and when we need that energy, we find it's not there. Consistently demanding energy from ourselves in this way can cause tremendous tiredness; it's like we are fighting ourselves. In this situation, sitting and resting to get your energy back can seem like a wonderful idea.

However, while you are sitting and resting, the unconscious and your habits that lie there are all still pulling on the available energy that's in your body. It's as if you have a bucket with several holes in it. The water is leaking out the sides and your solution is to fill the bucket with more water. So you keep putting more water in the top, but the water keeps going out—and you are running out of water. When does the madness end?

Well, first of all, seal up the holes. Start the process of completing things that you have left undone. Say, "I'm finished with that." "I'm not going to do that." "That's done." "No, I'm not going to do that one either. Sorry." But for this approach to work, you have to absolutely mean what you say.

It's important to keep in mind that energy follows thought. Even if the thought isn't complete, the energy keeps going. And the energy doesn't care about your good intentions. So when you say you are finished with a half-read book that's been lying around for months, don't feel cheated that you didn't get out of it what you wanted. You weren't getting anything out of it while it was lying around, anyway! It was draining you of your energy.

Now at least you've gone through an action of completeness, and one tiny leak has been sealed.

Keep going.

*When you judge another, you do not
define them; you define yourself.*

Wayne Dyer

No Need to Defend.

There is an old Sufi teaching that when a stranger or friend spreads negative or harmful rumors about you, you don't reply. You save the energy you would have expended in defending your name and allow your spiritual energy to increase.

When you win an argument, it means that someone else lost. If you are loving that person, you are then part of the loss. If you are not loving that person, you have lost in the bigger picture.

For me, if there is a conflict with another human being and someone declares it a win-lose situation, I'd choose the loss. I'd rather lose my ego, my position, my need to be right than win. I'd rather that someone I love learn from their winning than that I inflict a loss on them.

When it comes right down to it, there is no such thing as winning or losing. There is only experience. If I act out of integrity and loving, it doesn't matter who is right. It doesn't even matter what happens. What does matter is what I have invested inwardly. If I am attached to my limitations and my history of the past (which weigh down the present moment), I have lost the war even if I win the battle. If instead I present myself and my point of view in loving, with no attachment to the outcome, I have won before any battle has started.

Understanding is our strength. Being strong is not our strength. Being strong could mean resistance, and resistance could lead to separation. Strength is the understanding of our reality, and neither needs defense nor is fearful about an attack of others' opinions. When we truly stand in our strength, we transcend any win-lose situation.

You do not need to leave your room...
Remain sitting at your table and listen.
Do not even listen,
simply wait.
Do not even wait,
be quite still and solitary.
The world will freely offer itself
to you to be unmasked.
It has no choice.
It will roll in ecstasy at your feet.

Franz Kafka

Transcending Fear

Fear is such a funny thing. You should laugh at it rather than stand back in awe of it, making it sacred, and worshiping it—because there is nothing there. Fear is an illusion. It's just a word. Sure, a feeling goes along with it, but so what? Big deal. After you are done allowing fear to have power over you, you still have to go on with your life. You still go on living whether or not you are experiencing fear. So just drop the fear. One good way to do just that is to say, "I'd like the Mystical Traveler to handle that, please." Or, if you're really panicked, you can just say, "Traveler," and that might work the same way. It's been known to move fear out of the way and replace it with love and Light.

Fear can sometimes have a positive element, so it isn't always to be disregarded. If you fear failure, you might create success because you will put forth great effort to overcome what you fear. If you are fearful of reincarnation, you might do your spiritual exercises and free yourself from this level. If you handle fear in the right way, it can be positive and uplifting. A spiritual principle that I return to often is that everything can be used for your upliftment, learning, and growth—that includes when you are feeling fearful.

You also do not have to allow the word fear to shake you up. Words are a form of expression, but they are not reality. You don't have to let words upset you. Practically, however, I don't suppose there's anyone on the planet who can't be a little shaken by words. But it's how long you let those words shake you that needs to be your level of concern. It is an indicator of your spiritual growth and maturity when you can say, "Those words bothered me; I didn't care for them," and then move to the next thing.

The idea here is to transcend the consciousness of limitation. Whether limited by words or your own feelings, if you dwell in limitation, you dwell in poverty somewhere inside. To transcend, you draw to yourself what you need in order to see where you are inside, and then you lift above that. In other words, if you have been shaken by words in the past, you may continue to draw that level of hurt to you until you can learn to transcend and clear yourself of that limitation. That is why I recommend for you to reside in the Beloved. From there you transcend all limitations from a place of unconditional loving.

What we can or cannot do, what we consider possible or impossible, is rarely a function of our true capability. It is more likely a function of our beliefs about who we are.

Tony Robbins

Beliefs

You can try to destroy the ego. You can attempt to eliminate your desires. You can want to sacrifice the self. And when you've got through doing those three approaches, that's all you've got—those three approaches. Because you're not living the love that you are, which is the divine.

I don't care what path you are on or what path you study, or what kind of techniques or spiritual exercises you know. If you're not loving as you do it, you do nothing.

People think they are really growing when they see the aura around people with lights, colors, and forms. My comment is, "Is that all? Didn't you love them?" They usually say, " Oh, I forgot."

There is no value in the idiocy of looking at auras, lights, colors, or anything else without loving them. And if you are loving them, you don't care if you see anything else. For love will see itself. And love will do itself. All you do is sit there and let it radiate through you.

That's how you recognize a spiritual person. They will just let the loving radiate through them. That's the process of living love. That's the total path. It is not the path of destroying the ego, destroying desires, destroying the mind, becoming a fanatic. Because after you rip off all the layers, underneath is the loving layer. That is the very essence; it's the conducting of the divine. When you're doing that, you are sitting right in the center of creation. Whether you see it or not has nothing at all to do about it, you are that very foundation, the focal point upon which things revolve.

In the depth of my soul
there is a wordless song.

Kahlil Gibran

Spiritual Exercises

When practicing the Sound Current and riding this wave of God's energy and the Light that is with that, we have to look for where it is, not for where we would like it to be. It is where it is.

Listen, not just hear, but listen. That means you need to be very attentive to perceive audibly what is present at the true center of your being. Then you may hear the sound current of God.

To know God, to see God, to worship God, to praise God is man's ultimate destiny. It's not a destination, where you do it and then you stop. It's a destiny, meaning a continual ongoing practice that offers no reward except finding and worshiping and seeing and loving God as God. Not as the figment of your imagination, nor as the mythology you have created, but as it is. Everyone is going to find that. Why delay?

If there is to be any peace,
it will come through being,
not having.

Henry Miller

The Correct Altitude

There is a story told of a spiritual teacher in India who had a devotee who was going to leave the ashram and go out into the world. The teacher started enthusiastically praising him for all his goodness. And the devotee said, "Why did you tell me all those things? I know it's not true." The teacher replied, "You are not aware of it now, but that's what's true inside of you."

In the same way, the Beloved always sees what's inside of you, not as a probability and a possibility, but as that true potential that will come forward if it's watered enough with love and Light and encouragement. You can give that love and Light and encouragement to yourself by simply holding yourself in the highest regard, not as a performance in the world (that's the ego parading again) but as a knowing that you are the Beloved.

Right now the Beloved, that very thing that you have been looking for and praying for, is present. Many people pass it by because they don't think they are worthy. There is no need to create unworthiness in the midst of plenty. There is no need to feel that you're not worthy to eat at the harvest you've prayed into creation.

If there is something within you that is overriding your awareness or your divine communion with the Beloved, then observe that, for it has no place in the Kingdom of God. Gently and sensitively be with whatever is in the way, and observe the pattern, the feeling, the thinking, and what surfaces. If you stay with that, patiently observing more deeply, the answer becomes apparent, obvious, because it was always there. And you wonder how you could have missed it for so long.

When you observe neutrally, you can see what is in the way of knowing the Beloved as a living reality. You see what it truly

is and its relationship to everything else. Sometimes you need to get some distance by looking at it from a higher level. When you are far enough away from it, you see why you couldn't see it—you were just too close to it!

As you stay in that altitude, your loving floods the situation; you cannot help it, for the Beloved is in your very act of observation.

*The soul grows by its
constant participation
in that which transcends it.*

Gregory of Nyssa

Love More Each Day

Who needs God when every-
thing is fine? Everything is fine, that is God. Who needs God
when God is present? God is doing it all. Yet we cry out, "Oh,
God, help me." It's true that God is most amazing when you're at
your worst because we notice the miracles more. In reality, the
miracles are all around us in every moment.

The living miracle is found in the consciousness of the
Beloved that resides within each person. There you can move
through space, time, energy, and matter into the timeless,
formless, spaceless sphere that is called the Soul. You don't lose
your identity. You replace your personality with the correct
identity of who you truly are.

Divine Communion is being present in the Beloved while
you are with the person in front of you, unconditionally loving
them. Then, being with the next person and unconditionally
loving them—then the person next to them and sharing your
loving with that one. You'll find you can't wait to keep doing it.
And the only reason you separate for a few minutes is to get a
glass of water and something to eat in order to build the energy
to come back and do it all over again. Time means nothing.
Space means nothing. And whether you're twenty or eighty
years old, you are with the one you love, and you're in that
divine moment.

In that Divinity, no matter where someone goes or what
they do, you're in communion with them. We do have physical
bodies and we like to see other's physical bodies, and we like to
touch their Souls by way of their body. We like to feel that love
and their lips and to share their food. But even as we enjoy it, it's
very important we not focus just on their physicality, but that we
instead focus on our love in that sharing. Our love is inside of us

and that same love is inside of others, in that awareness and attention is the Divine Communion.

There is a song with lyrics that say,

> *"I'm going to love more each day,*
> *I'm going to give more than I take,*
> *I'm going to live more for the sake, of living love."*

Those words are a beautiful affirmation that I recommend you use.

When you do live love, everything becomes fantastic. You manifest here and now and receive God's Grace. You bestow Grace upon yourself from a higher consciousness. Then you are the Beloved.

The lesson which life repeats and constantly enforces is "look under foot." You are always nearer the divine and the true sources of your power than you think. The lure of the distant and the difficult is deceptive. The great opportunity is where you are. Do not despise your own place and hour. Every place is under the stars, every place is the center of the world.

John Burroughs

The Presence of the Christ

The Christ is not a religion, a tradition, or even any kind of spiritual path. It's a breath, a breath of the Divine. You really do breathe in the Divine essence that is the consciousness of the Christ. It is unique and it is extremely sacred.

Because space and time are not applicable in terms of the Spirit, you already are all that you will become. All you have to do is claim your heritage. The Soul is entirely present, right now. All you need do is awaken to that level.

You are the only one who can delay or block your progress. You are the only one who can cloud your awareness. By the same token, you are the only one who can recognize the Christ within. You are the one who can make the Beloved a living reality in your life and who can demonstrate the unconditional loving and forgiveness that indicate the presence of the Christ.

If you wish to make a man happy,
add not unto his riches but take away
from his desires.

Epicurus

Walk in Grace

If you think that being the Beloved is going to give you everything you want in this world, you have missed the point. The Beloved is a desireless state. You will get everything you want when you are in complete acceptance, cooperation, understanding, and empathy for whatever is present. But the wants that are being fulfilled are not the wants of the emotions but the wants of the heart. And as soon as a "but" appears in your mind you have stepped out of the energy field of the Beloved and have thrust yourself into the world again. Don't be concerned, for the Beloved waits for your return.

You can return to the Beloved on your breath, on your gratitude, on your loving, and on your unconditional giving. There are many ways into the Beloved when you are prepared to let go and let God. Your reward will be the enthusiasm you have for your life regardless of your circumstances. You will walk in Grace. And the Grace of God did not say for one moment that you wouldn't have any pain, or that you won't meet any adversity. Its only promise is that you are going to live in the Spirit while you walk through this world.

In music, in a flower, in a leaf, in an act of kindness... I see what people call God in all these things.

Pablo Casals

Sometimes Non-Doing Is the Answer.

We can be in a state of doing, or we can be in a state of being. In a state of being, we don't have to do anything. All we have to do is just be here.

We're always doing something, for good or for bad, as a necessity of our life. Then we let these necessities become our focus. But when you live in the Beloved, being just expresses itself through you as limitless love and energy.

If we can just be, and we can let that being of who we are come forward, this being will do away with all the doing that has been our compulsive and obsessive behavior. Then our being does the doing. And there's no karma because the action is done from the state of being, not from the state of ego, or from right and wrong or anything else like that.

Your conditioning says that you've got to be doing something. But when you're sitting in the divine presence of the Beloved, it all becomes very humorous because it's all Spirit. The joke is your separation. Laugh. It will do you good.

We do not live merely to "do something"—no matter what. We do not live more fully merely by doing more, seeing more, tasting more, and experiencing more than we ever have before. On the contrary, some of us need to discover that we will not begin to live more fully until we have the courage to do and see and taste and experience much less than usual.

Thomas Merton

The Ease of Grace

You enter into Grace by loving God. Once you start to love God, Grace is always present. Living in Grace is not hard. If it's starting to be hard, you're under the law. Giving up the struggle of going for Grace might be the very thing that releases you to experience it. Grace isn't something that you go for as much as it's something you allow. However, you may not know Grace is present, because you have conditioned the way you want it to come, for example, like thunder or lightning, with all the drama, rumbling, and pretense of that. In fact, Grace comes in very naturally, like breathing.

When you receive Grace it becomes an attitude, a way of being, that you maintain. One way to do this is to hold a picture in your mind that you want more of, one that uplifts you. Once the attitude is formed, it is then practiced as a conscious behavior. The body then takes over and incorporates it as a habit. We then start to walk through life not even knowing that we're Grace-filled and joyful until people notice and bring it to our attention. You're joyful because you are not preoccupied with the things that used to bother you. They're still there but they don't bother you because you don't focus on them.

With Grace nothing leaves your life. You haven't given up your mind or your experiences. You're not brainwashing yourself into some oblivion. It's just that you're focusing on what is really important to you. You are choosing a lifestyle and a behavior that brings you freedom. However, like all human beings (including Lot's wife), we have a tendency to look back. When we do, we often become paralyzed by what we see. There is no need to look back, there is no need to look anywhere except where you are. To maintain being in a state of Grace, just be in a state of forgiveness, which is a place of no judgment.

Historically, we can see that those human beings who lived in a state of Grace, as a statement of their life, became saints. My point of view is that if you're putting up with this planet and living here, you're a saint already. When you live in a state of Grace, when you want to tell somebody, "Up yours," the words come out differently. People sense the Grace you are extending to them when you really had all the right and authority to have laid them low. However, you withheld the striking out, and Grace went in its place. That's the forgiving that continues on as you maintain your loving connection. You will not finish up forgiving until your last breath.

Our judgments of our past keep us tied to this world. When we're through with our work on this planet, in our last moments, our forgiveness will be, "I forgive myself for all this," and then the name of God will be the next thing we utter.

*Meister Eckhart radically revises the
whole notion of spiritual programs.
He says that there is no such thing as
a spiritual journey. If a little shocking,
this is refreshing. If there were a
spiritual journey, it would be only a
quarter inch long, though many miles
deep. It would be a swerve into rhythm
with your deeper nature and presence.
The wisdom here is so consoling.
You do not have to go way outside
yourself to come into real conversation
with your soul and with the mysteries
of the spiritual world. The eternal is
at home—within you.*

John O'Donohue

A Walking Prayer Answered

If you don't know how to differentiate between Jesus the Christ, Buddha, Krishna, the Mystical Traveler, the Holy Spirit, or God, you don't really need to. Just call it the Beloved. Because that's what it is. That's what I call it—the Beloved. If you call it "The Lover" then that means there's also a loved one, so there are two. But in the energy field of which I speak, there are not two, there is no other, there's just one, for the Beloved includes all.

We can look at the Beloved as being where the inner worlds and the outer worlds meet. However, in reality, there is no inner or outer as much as there is a continuum. It's simply just a flowing in and a flowing out, and it's often very difficult to know which was inner and which was outer. But if you are in the presence of the Beloved, there's so much joy that it just doesn't seem to matter.

To establish your connection to the Beloved, take time for yourself. Time for your Self is not watching TV or going to the movies, it's removing yourself from your usual distractions so you can sit down and in the silence call upon God's presence and do spiritual exercises. As you close your eyes, this energy of the Beloved starts to love and adore you. This loving and adoration draws you more and more into itself and you come to a serenity that most people won't understand. It is not a mental thing. It's not the word, "happy." It is an energy field that is by itself absolutely whole and complete. It is called God, the divine nature of the Beloved.

Within this energy field, you reside in a state of knowing. First you feel you're the Beloved. Then you know you're the Beloved. Finally, you just are the Beloved, and you become a walking prayer answered. You actually become the savior or the

anointed one to everyone whom even your shadow falls upon. Because even the shadow carries the radiant energy of the Beloved as it radiates out from you. It is not an ego statement; it's a statement of being the Beloved.

In this energy field as you walk by people and look at them, they'll say, "My God, I feel so much better, why?" Because the Soul, the divine, God, just looked at them. In this sacred place it seems that all good things come your way—not all the material things you want—all good things come your way. How you use those things is up to you and how you use your personal talent. If you've been able to handle money, you'll handle the money that comes to you very well. If you've been a spendthrift, and money comes in, it will go out as fast as it ever has because the Beloved doesn't make you talented in this world. It infuses divinity here.

Don Juan: "To seek freedom is the only driving force I know. Freedom to fly off into that infinity out there. Freedom to dissolve; to lift off; to be like the flame of the candle, which, in spite of being up against the light of a billion stars, remains intact, because it never pretended to be more than what it is: a mere candle."

Carlos Castaneda

Ordinariness: A Prior Condition to God

Hopefully we're all being teachers and lovers and the Beloved to each other and holding a loving attitude with each other, so if somebody goes to fall, we can support them. And should they actually fall, we can pick them up and be there for them until they get their feet back on the ground. In loving, we can handle life's ups and downs without drama, in a natural, flowing, ordinary way.

I can recall a lifetime in India where I was being taken to see a great spiritual master. Although it was a lengthy boat ride to see him, I was being treated royally. There were garlands of flowers around me, and I sat comfortably at the back of the boat where there was shade and cushions, while several servants did the rowing. When we reached shore, I was helped up the mountain to where the master resided. My baggage was carried for me, and the place where I slept overnight was luxurious and I was fed a magnificent meal. I got to see the master the next day and he initiated me.

When it came time to return to the boat, I noticed that I had to carry my own bags. When I stepped into the boat, I was ushered past the shaded part of the boat to the front where I was given an oar to row the boat. I couldn't believe it—they had me rowing the boat back to shore.

When we arrived at the shore they had me stay with the boat. Someone came on board, sat at the back of the boat, and was surrounded by garlands of flowers. I along with a few others had to row this new person back to the place where the master resided.

I had a lot of resistance and resentment going on inside of me, but when I looked at the other rowers around me, they all had a smile. As I looked at them, I spontaneously broke into

riotous laughter for I suddenly realized why the other rowers were smiling. It was because on the return ride, this new person at the back of the boat, in the shade surrounded by flowers, was going to be rowing.

From that point on, I have never had it inside of me that one role in life is greater than any other. It's simply that we're all doing different things at different times. There are times when I fall and people pick me up. And there are times when others fall and I assist picking them up. But we are all, in one way or another, rowing the boat because we are all in it.

There is no need for comparison or envy when we encounter someone who thinks they're so wonderful and great, because we can all smile in the knowledge that they are going to be part of the ordinariness before too long. The Beloved eventually reduces us all to ordinariness, because ordinariness is the prior condition to God.

*When searching for harmony in life,
one must never forget that in the
drama of existence we are ourselves
both actors and spectators.*

Niels Bohr

God Supplies the Melody, You Produce the Words

There are so many names for God. It won't make any difference to the God I know because He's none of those. He's That Which Is. So when you speak, That Which Is listens and responds by using anyone of us.

It is really hard to get close to God when God is you and you are God. It's very hard to know the difference. The only way we can know the difference is to stand back and judge and curse and plead and beg for a sign that God is recognizing and loving us. We put up big churches and temples and cathedrals and synagogues to go somewhere to pray to God, when they are just symbols of the separation of us from God. However, if we really need to go into a building to bring us back to knowing that God is immediately present—as peace is present, as you are present—then let's do that.

God does not supply you materiality. God supplies you with the harmonics—the ability to be in harmony. God supplies a melody and you produce the words. God supplies the air and you breathe it. God supplies the love and you partake of it.

God is a God of nowness, of immediacy, of this moment. The one I just spoke about a second ago is not the same one I'm talking about now, because that one is in the past. Nor is God in the future except that he goes from the beginning through to the end. So God's presence is in my past, in my present, and in my future. That means I'm a secure individual. Life is all wrapped up for me.

Does that mean I'm going to get mine? I've got God. I don't care what mine is. It can be any number of things, and it can also be nothing. It doesn't matter. It is all the same because it is God that I'm keeping my eyes on, not a physical form. The God that I keep my eyes on is loving, and I keep my eyes on the loving.

Then I see who is loving and they become the Beloved—the lover and the loved become one because they are exercising God's love.

Are you continually resurrecting
the joy of your Spirit within you?

Are you allowing space inside of
you for regeneration and renewal?

Are you taking time for what
is most important in your life?

If the answer is no, you didn't get it.

If yes, you are well on your way
and you will keep transforming.

And one day, you will look at yourself in a mirror
and see the one you've been looking for:

The Beloved.

 John-Roger, D.S.S.

Meditation CD

Included at the back of this book is a meditation CD with fourteen tracks. In the first track, John-Roger takes us through a breathing exercise, with a lot of humor, to bring more Spirit into our bodies. This is done primarily through exhaling in specfic way that opens up space in the lungs while releasing toxins. The exhale is a gentle and slow blowing action where the cheeks may puff up but the air is allowed out slowly and without any force being used. In tracks 2–13, Paul Kaye reads some of the more meditative chapters of the book. This is a time to just listen, let go, and allow yourself to relax into the Beloved. Track 14 is another breathing exercise by John-Roger in which he guides us into following the rising and falling of our breath. Amazingly, in under 4 minutes John-Roger guides us to a deep place of peace within us. You will probably want to play this track every day, either to begin your day in peace and calm or as a relaxing completion to the day.

CD tracks include:

[1] **Breathing Exercise**
John-Roger, D.S.S. (4:50)

[2] **In the Now**
Paul Kaye, D.S.S. (6:47)

[3] **Divine Communion**
Paul Kaye, D.S.S. (3:53)

[4] **The Sound of God**
Paul Kaye, D.S.S. (5:31)

[5] **A Moment of Silence**
Paul Kaye, D.S.S. (3:52)

[6] **Letting Go of the Past**
Paul Kaye, D.S.S. (4:26)

[7] **Wealthy Beyond Measure**
Paul Kaye, D.S.S. (3:09)

[8] **With the Beloved**
Paul Kaye, D.S.S. (3:16)

[9] **Unconditional Loving**
Paul Kaye, D.S.S. (4:45)

[10] **Attuning to the Beloved**
Paul Kaye, D.S.S. (4:08)

[11] **Doing Nothing**
Paul Kaye, D.S.S. (5:06)

[12] **The Song of the Beloved**
Paul Kaye, D.S.S. (5:31)

[13] **Entering Into Grace**
Paul Kaye, D.S.S. (2:55)

[14] **Breathing and Peace**
John-Roger, D.S.S. (3:43)

Quotations

The quotations contained in the book came from many diverse sources. Some have been in our personal collections for many years, and are from sources we have long forgotten. If you know of the source of any unattributed quotation, we will happily acknowledge them in future editions of the book. The Internet provides a rich source of material. We are grateful to the following, for quotations we have found on their Internet sites:

charityfocus.org, thinkexist.com, wisdomquotes.com, quotes.zaadz.com, herondance.org

We are also extremely grateful to the following for permission to use their work:

Just Sit There Right Now – **Hafiz**
From the Penguin anthology*Love Poems to God*
Copyright© 2002 Daniel Ladinsky, used by his permission; p. 176
Penguin Group, ISBN: 0142196126
Penguin Putnam Inc., 375 Hudson Street, New York, NY 10014

The Guest House – **Rumi**
The Essential Rumi by Coleman Barks; p. 109
Harper San Francisco (now Harper One), ISBN: 978-0062509581
HarperCollins Publishers, 10 East 53rd Street, NY, NY 10022

Three **Jack Gilbert** quotes:
Refusing Heaven by Jack Gilbert
i) PAGE 18; ii) PAGE 3; iii) PAGE 19
Alfred A. Knopf, ISBN: 978-0375710858
Random House, Inc., Copyright and Permissions Department
1745 Broadway, New York, NY 10019
randomhouse.com/knopf/poetry

Additional Resources and Study Materials by John-Roger, D.S.S.

The following books and materials can support you in learning more about the ideas presented in The Rest of Your Life. To order the books, CDs and DVDs, please contact MSIA at 1-800-899-2665, order@msia.org, or simply visit our online store at www.msia.org. John-Roger's books are also available at bookstores everywhere.

Momentum: Letting Love Lead — Simple Practices for Spiritual Living (with Paul Kaye, D.S.S.)

As much as we might like to have the important areas of our lives—Relationships, Health, Finances and Career—all settled and humming along, the reality for most of us is that there is always *something* out of balance, often causing stress and distress. Rather than resisting or regretting imbalance, this book shows that there is an inherent *wisdom* in imbalance. Where there is imbalance, there is movement, and that movement "gives rise to a dynamic, engaging life that is full of learning, creativity, and growth."

We can discover—in the very areas where we experience most of our problems and challenges—the greatest movement and the greatest opportunity for change.

The approach is not to try harder at making life work. Life already works. The big key is to bring loving into it. This book is about being loving in the moment. It is a course in loving.

Hardbound book #1893020185, $19.95

When Are You Coming Home? A personal guide to Soul Transcendence (with Pauli Sanderson, D.S.S.)

An intimate account of spiritual awakening that contains the elements of an adventure story. How did John-Roger attain the awareness of who he truly is? He approached life like a scientist in a laboratory. He found methods for integrating the sacred with the mundane, the practical with the mystical. He noted what worked and what didn't. Along with some fascinating stories, you will find in this book many practical keys for making your own life work better, for attuning to the source of wisdom that is always within you, and for making every day propel you further on your exciting adventure home.

Hardbound book # 189302023, $19.95

What's It Like Being You? (with Paul Kaye, D.S.S.)

"What would happen if you stopped doing what you thought you were supposed to be doing and started being who you are?" The sequel to their previous book together, Momentum—Letting Love Lead, this book features exercises, meditations and narrative to deepen and explore who you really are as well as a new CD release "Meditation for Alignment with the True Self".

Softbound book #:1-893020-25-8, $14.95

Spiritual Warrior: The Art of Spiritual Living

Full of wisdom, humor, common sense, and hands-on tools for spiritual living, this book offers practical tips to take charge of our lives and create greater health, happiness, abundance, and loving. Becoming a spiritual warrior has nothing to do with violence. It is about using the positive qualities of the spiritual warrior—intention, ruthlessness, and impeccability—to counter negative personal habits and destructive relationships, especially when you are confronted with great adversity.

Hardbound book #01482936X, $20

The Tao of Spirit

This beautifully designed collection of writings is intended to free you from outer worldly distractions and guide your return to the stillness within. The *Tao of Spirit* can provide daily inspirations and new approaches on how to handle stress and frustration. What a wonderful way to start or to end the day— remembering to let go of your day-to-day problems and be refreshed in the source at the center of your existence. Many people use this book in preparation for meditation or prayer.

Hardbound book #0914829335, $15

Forgiveness: The Key to the Kingdom

Forgiveness is the key factor in personal liberation and spiritual progression. This book presents profound insights into forgiveness and the resulting personal joy and freedom. God's business is forgiving. This book provides encouragement and techniques for making it our business as well.

Softbound Book #0914829629, $12.95

Inner Worlds of Meditation

In this self-help guide to meditation, meditation practices are transformed into valuable and practical resources for exploring the spiritual realms and dealing with life more effectively. Included are a variety of meditations that can be used for gaining spiritual awareness, achieving greater relaxation, balancing the emotions, and increasing energy.

Softbound Book #0914829459, $11.95
3-CD packet #0914829645, $30

Loving Each Day for Peacemakers: Choosing Peace Every Day

Peace? It's a noble idea, yet a seemingly elusive reality. Peace between nations is built upon peace between individuals, and peace between individuals depends upon peace within each person. Making peace more than just a theory or idea, *Loving Each Day For Peacemakers* guides readers to their own solutions for experiencing peace.

Hardbound book #1893020142, $12

Psychic Protection

In this book, John-Roger describes some of the invisible levels: the power of thoughts, the unconscious, elemental energies, and magic. More important, he discusses how to protect yourself against negativity that can be part of those levels. As you practice the simple techniques in this book, you can create a greater sense of well-being in and around you.

Softbound Book #0914829696, $6.95

Turning Points to Personal Liberation

John-Roger presents direct, insightful information outlining the causes and cures of hurt, anger, confusion, jealousy, feelings of separation and loneliness, and other limiting behaviors and beliefs that often block our happiness, success and enjoyment. These CDs contain practical keys and wisdom for gaining greater acceptance, understanding, loving, freedom, and liberation:

Keys to Handling Negative Emotions
Turning Hurt and Anger to Acceptance and Loving
5 Characteristics and Cures of Emotional Mood Swings
Ten of life's essential questions
Insecurity and what to do about it
Healing the Hurt.

7-CD set # 1893020452, $30

Health From the Inside Out

This set of three CDs outlines how to use the energy of the body to create better health. Included are insights into the cycle of overeating and practical methods for overcoming it. There is a description of how to use the power of thought for better health, as well as to connect with the Supreme Source to promote greater healing and vitality. These CDs also describe how we sometimes promote "dis-ease" and how to change those patterns to gain better physical balance.

Topics on the CDs include:

Adapting towards health or adopting dis-ease
Are you stuffing your expression?
Are you unconsciously depleting your energy?
Awakening beyond body consciousness
Body balance meditation

3-CD set # 1893020401, $25

Observation, The Key to Letting Go

In order to accept what is, we need to observe, like a scientist. "Observation," John-Roger says, "is the key to letting go and letting God." In observation, we are not getting involved with our emotions or bringing preconceived assumptions to the situation. Learning how to practice these principles more effectively can have tangible and profound benefits for bringing greater balance and happiness into our lives.

CD #1552, $10

Are You Available to Yourself?

Health, wealth, happiness, abundance, and riches are our heritage in this life. John-Roger reminds us that everything is available to us if we are available to ourselves and the spiritual life-force within us all.

CD #7238-CD, $10
DVD #7238-DVD, $20

Soul Awareness Discourses—
A Course in Soul Transcendence

Soul Awareness Discourses are designed to teach Soul Transcendence, which is becoming aware of yourself as a Soul and as one with God, not as a theory, but as a living reality. They are for people who want a consistent, time-proven approach to their spiritual enfoldment.

A set of Soul Awareness Discourses consists of 12 booklets, one to study and contemplate each month of the year. As you read each Discourse, you can activate an awareness of your Divine essence and deepen your relationship with God.

Spiritual in essence, Discourses are compatible with religious beliefs you might hold. In fact, most people find that Discourses support the experience of whatever path, philosophy, or religion (if any) they choose to follow. Simply put, Discourses are about eternal truths and the wisdom of the heart.

The first year of Discourses addresses topics ranging from creating success in the world to working hand-in-hand with Spirit.

A yearly set of Discourses is regularly $100. MSIA is offering the first year of Discourses at an introductory price of $50. Discourses come with a full, no-questions-asked, money-back guarantee. If at any time you decide this course of study is not right for you, simply return it, and you will promptly receive a full refund.

To order Discourses, contact the Movement of Spiritual Inner Awareness at 1-800-899-2665, order@msia.org or visit www.msia.org

About the Authors

John-Roger, D.S.S.

A teacher and lecturer of international stature, John-Roger is an inspiration in the lives of many people around the world. For over four decades, his wisdom, humor, common sense and love have helped people to discover the Spirit within themselves and find health, peace, and prosperity.

With two co-authored books on the New York Times Bestseller list to his credit, and more than three dozen spiritual and self-help books and audio albums, John-Roger offers extraordinary insights on a wide range of topics. He is the founder of the Church of the Movement of Spiritual Inner Awareness (MSIA), which focuses on Soul Transcendence; founder and Chancellor of the University of Santa Monica; founder and President of Peace Theological Seminary & College of Philosophy; founder and chairman of the board of Insight Seminars; and founder and President of The Institute for Individual & World Peace.

John-Roger has given over 6,000 lectures and seminars worldwide, many of which are televised nationally on his cable program, "That Which Is," through the Network of Wisdoms. He has appeared on numerous radio and television shows and been a featured guest on "Larry King Live".

An educator and minister by profession, John-Roger continues to transform lives by educating people in the wisdom of the spiritual heart.

For more information about John-Roger, you may also visit:
www.john-roger.org

Paul Kaye, D.S.S.

Paul Kaye has been a dedicated student of spiritual thought and practices since his youth in England. His explorations have taken him into Yoga, Zen, and the spiritual foundations of movement and the martial arts.

Paul's interests include the philosophies of such poets and teachers as Lao Tzu, Rumi and Kabir and the esoteric teachings of Jesus Christ. Paul has designed workshops on the practical application of spiritual principles and presented them worldwide. Paul is a unique and remarkable presence. He brings an abundance of lightheartedness into whatever he does, and his presentations are inspiring, practical, and filled with a wonderful sense of humor and wisdom.

For over 35 years he has studied with renowned educator and author John-Roger and he is president of the Church of the Movement of Spiritual Inner Awareness (MSIA), an ecumenical, non-denominational church. Paul is an ordained minister and has a Doctorate in Spiritual Science.

For Author Interviews and Speaking Engagements

Please contact Angel Gibson at:
Mandeville Press
3500 West Adams blvd.
Los Angeles, CA 90018
323-737-4055 x 155
angel@mandevillepress.org

We welcome your comments and questions.

Mandeville Press
P.O. Box 513935
Los Angeles, CA 90051-1935 USA
323-737-4055
jrbooks@mandevillepress.org
www.mandevillepress.org

LaVergne, TN USA
28 May 2010
184176LV00001B/2/P